The Knowable Past

by

Kenneth J. Dillon

Scientia Press

All Rights Reserved

Printed in the U.S.A.

September 2018

© Kenneth J. Dillon, 2018

Publisher's Cataloguing in Publication

Dillon, Kenneth J.

    The Knowable Past / Kenneth J. Dillon
    196 p.; ill.; 23 cm. Contains index.
    D6.B25 2018 | 907'.2
    1. History—General. 2. History—Ancient. 3. History—United States. 4. History—Modern. 5. Planetology. 6. Earth—History. 7. Velikovsky, Immanuel, 1895-1979. 8. Quigley, Carroll, 1910-1977. 9. Conspiracy theories. 10. Terrorism. I. Title
    ISBN: 9780964297685
    Library of Congress Control Number: 2017917737

Cover design by Navid Marvi

Scientia Press
Washington, D.C.
www.scientiapress.com

In memory of my father

James Dillon

[W]hen a *fact* appears to be opposed to a long train of *deductions*, it *invariably* proves to be capable of bearing some *other interpretation*.

Arthur Conan Doyle

Contents

Preface……………………………………………..…………………………..3

Chapter 1. Jupiter, Venus, and Velikovsky…………………………………….5

Chapter 2. The Outer Solar System Origin of the Terrestrial Planets………..15

Chapter 3. The Martian Theory of Mass Extinctions……………………....32

Chapter 4. Theory of the Reversing Earth……………………………….41

Chapter 5. Evidence from Egypt……………………………...……………….48

Chapter 6. Venus, the Ancient Near East, and Islam………………………..64

Chapter 7. Why Topless? Why the Snakes?..72

Chapter 8. Catastrophes and Climate Change in Ancient China…………..78

Chapter 9. Venus, Skeleton Key to Stonehenge……………………………88

Chapter 10. Venus in the Americas…………………………...……..95

Chapter 11. The Trojan Origin of Roman Civilization…………….………..102

Chapter 12. Strategic Mistakes of World Wars I and II………….………111

Chapter 13. Carroll Quigley, Theorist of Civilizations………………..….118

Chapter 14. Did the KGB Arrange the Assassination of John F. Kennedy?.124

Chapter 15. Prying the Lids off the 2001 Cover-ups…………….………138

Chapter 16. Was Abderraouf Jdey the Anthrax Mailer?............................142

Chapter 17. Conclusion...167

Further Reading..183

Photo Credits...186

Index..187

About the Author..194

Preface

What is the Knowable Past?

Every historical puzzle has information associated with it, perhaps enough to solve it. That doesn't mean that we will solve it, but it does suggest that some unsolved puzzles are ripe for solving if we can just figure out the right approach. Famous crimes like the assassination of President John F. Kennedy have generated so much evidence and so many theories that some people say "We'll never solve that one." Yet the presence of a good deal of evidence might instead lead us to wonder whether someone has actually already solved the problem, but people are ignoring or rejecting the solution.

Of course, some cases we will never solve—though how do we know which ones these are? With others we must content ourselves with "more likely than not" or "much more likely than not" solutions—90% sure? Or so much evidence will accumulate that reasonable observers will say "It must be true" even though the proof is not watertight. Are these cases 98% sure? Hard to tell, but still useful to have some degree of certitude.

In this book I argue that *the solutions to quite a few seemingly mysterious or unknowable problems of history are knowable, and some are in fact known.* In other words, in contradistinction to the commonly known Past, the Knowable Past includes problems that could be solved with our current information as well as solved problems whose solutions have been ignored.

I also extend the word "history" to include planetary and Earth science. As historical sciences, these bear the hallmark of history in that they are contingent on past events that leave evidence behind, even if that evidence is not written testimony (but some of it is!).

Being a voluminous subject, the Past does not admit to comprehensive discussion in a single book like this. Even the various episodes appearing in these pages will receive only partial treatment. I aim simply to sketch out the problems, attempt to solve them, and draw a conclusion or two. In other words, this book offers historical and scientific detective work, with a bit of philosophy thrown in.

With the exception of Chapter 1, which seeks to resolve the Immanuel Velikovsky case discussed in the first ten chapters, we will follow chronological order. First will come Chapters 2-4 on episodes in planetary and Earth science. Then Chapters 5-10 will examine evidence from around the world on the Venus theory of the Bronze Age catastrophes. Chapter 11 sets forth another theory of ancient history, the Trojan Origin of Roman Civilization. Then we will make a great leap forward to modern times in Chapters 12-16, from the world wars to fatal events and remarkable people in modern America. In Chapter 17, we will draw lessons from the individual chapters, see how the various topics fit into more overarching themes, and reach some conclusions. Much of this material appeared first in a different form at www.scientiapress.com.

Why this particular odd mixture of topics? Because these are the ones to which I can add value! Why such emphasis on the Velikovsky/Venus-related topics? Because the Velikovsky case is the world's greatest ongoing instance of Scientific Rejectionism, because the process of trying to resolve it has generated so many intriguing findings, and because such important science and history are at stake. A brilliant interdisciplinary researcher, Velikovsky made plenty of pioneer's mistakes; but he also made remarkable discoveries.

Lastly, I would like to thank all those who contributed to my journey through these subjects. That includes in particular Ross Getman for the anthrax mailings case; Miao Li for ancient China; Andrea Hull for copyediting; Navid Marvi for the cover; John Brown, Tianyue Jiang, my sister Janet, and my brother Jim for editorial advice; and my students for their feedback and ideas. I must also thank hostile critics of me and my fellow researchers. By challenging us and correcting mistakes, they have made contributions to the progress of this enterprise!

Chapter 1

Jupiter, Venus, and Velikovsky

Figure 1. Immanuel Velikovsky

The publication in 1950 of Russian-American psychoanalyst Immanuel Velikovsky's *Worlds in Collision*[1] set off a bitter controversy that has continued in a muted and yet increasingly fruitful way since his death in 1979. Velikovsky argued that Venus had emerged as a comet from Jupiter and repeatedly approached Earth every 52 years, causing the devastating floods, droughts, volcanic eruptions, and earthquakes of the Bronze Age catastrophes (BAC). In the greatest controversy in planetary science since Copernicus and Galileo, critics stigmatized Velikovsky as a pseudoscientist, leading to such neglect of his work that today some planetary scientists have never even heard of him.

Now new evidence and reinterpretation show that in fact Velikovsky made several remarkable contributions. In a rush to judgment, his critics

---

[1] (New York: Macmillan, 1950), then (New York: Doubleday, 1950)

threw the baby out with the bathwater. And a revised and updated version of the Venus theory has led to other important scientific findings and theories while also explaining many anomalies in ancient history. Thus the Velikovsky case has much to teach us about planetary and Earth science, ancient history, and Scientific Rejectionism.

In the succeeding chapters of this book, we will examine the new findings and theories that have emerged. But let us start here by discussing first Velikovsky's life, then the controversy itself.

The Velikovsky Story

Born in 1895 and educated as a medical doctor in Russia[2], and briefly at European universities, Velikovsky migrated to Germany, where he met Albert Einstein, then to Palestine. He worked there from 1924 to 1939 as a medical doctor, and he also became a Freudian psychoanalyst. In 1939 he moved with his family to New York City, where he began researching at the Columbia University Library. Working across subject boundaries, Velikovsky developed theories about the planets in ancient times, sharing them with scientists. But they reacted strongly against his ideas. When he published *Worlds in Collision*, they threatened to boycott the publisher, Macmillan, so that it transferred the publication rights to Doubleday. The book went on to sell more than a million copies. In 1952 he moved to Princeton where he had contact with Einstein again.

Velikovsky published various other books, including *Earth in Upheaval*,[3] which examined the geological evidence that supported his catastrophist theory. He developed a detailed, radically foreshortened chronology of ancient history. He also argued that electromagnetic forces played a major role in the solar system. Largely shunned by scientists, he gradually gained a following among students and iconoclasts, leading to invitations to speak at universities. In 1974, at age 79, he skillfully and single-handedly debated multiple opponents at a session organized by the

---

[2] On the side he studied ancient history. His earlier education included reading the Torah in Hebrew.
[3] (New York: Doubleday, 1955)

American Association for the Advancement of Science and heavily stacked against him. Velikovsky died in Princeton in 1979.

A Tangled Controversy

Opponents found fault with dozens of details of Velikovsky's Venus scenario, above all with the notion that Venus had exploded out of Jupiter. The requisite rapid, unexplained circularization of Venus' orbit also drew their fire. In general, they argued that his theories violated the laws of science.

Meanwhile, several liberal arts academics came to Velikovsky's defense, devising refutations of the objections and hunting for evidence to support the theories.[4] They were joined by a multitude of Velikovsky supporters who saw the criticisms of him as a classic case of the scientific establishment suppressing new findings. Kept at arms' length by scientific journal editors, they formed discussion groups and published various books as well as a series of journals. Eventually the debate migrated to the Internet, where more findings and reinterpretations emerged.

Many factors contributed to making the debate over Velikovsky's theories especially complicated and bitter:

1. Both critics and defenders were partly right and partly wrong;
2. Personal antagonisms led to invective, driving the two camps to assert their views rigidly while completely dismissing the evidence and arguments of the other side;
3. A determined contrarian, Velikovsky ranged into fields where he lacked expertise and took provocative positions that tended to undermine his credibility. For instance, early on he speculated that Earth had orbited Saturn. Even though he then dropped this idea, his critics did not stop using it against him;

---

[4] Ancient historians remained silent, with the exception of historians of science, who took exception to Velikovsky's interpretations. However, one historian of science, Livio Stecchini, sided with him and made several useful contributions.

4. Some participants failed to distinguish between centrally important claims (and objections) and peripheral ones;
5. In a rush to judgment, critics failed to perceive that such novel, wide-ranging, and ambiguous subject matter required further research before arriving at conclusions;
6. Using their expertise, prestige, and control of journals, critical scientists, backed by professional skeptics, successfully stigmatized Velikovsky and his theory, thereby creating taboos that discouraged other scientists from researching the subject and eventually ended discussion of it in scientific journals;
7. The publicity and stigmatization stimulated other researchers to propose alternative theories (asteroid swarms, hypothetical planets, etc.), though these ignored the mass of evidence pointing to Venus and the smaller amount of evidence pointing to later approaches of Mars, thereby confusing the debate;
8. Velikovsky's publishing success led writers of science fiction and fantasy (e.g., Erich von Däniken and Zecharia Sitchin) to construct parallel scenarios, but with aliens and other unscientific material. Velikovsky—by many accounts a keen, serious, and hardworking investigator—was often lumped into the same category;
9. Even if electromagnetic forces are set aside, planetary approaches that involve the invisible gravitational force acting at a distance to cause tidal disruption are inherently more difficult to study and demonstrate than impacts and terrestrial factors; and
10. The Venus theory included extraordinary events, unusual phenomena, poorly characterized mechanisms, fragmentary data, and remarkable timing: after billions of years, just a few thousand years ago, and at the very time when humans could first report what they witnessed—but they did so in largely mythical terms!

Endless Objections

As years passed critics generated an ever-growing number of objections—including those of a counterfactual type (negative evidence). For instance, they argued that, if Earth had turned over during four especially close passages of Venus, as Velikovsky claimed based on what Herodotus reported that Egyptian priests had told him, the oceans would have completely flooded the land, yet there is no evidence of such a stupendous global flood. So they concluded that Velikovsky was wrong.

In fact, we can now see that the answer to this objection is that it depends on the *speed* of the inversion. A slower inversion would cause smaller but still great tsunamis and flooding, for which there is indeed evidence.

Perhaps without intending to do so, the critics came to engage in an Objection Game (often with an embedded Parameter Game) not unlike the allegation games that lawyers use in court. If Velikovsky supporters answered one objection, they would come up with another, and another, all of them distracting attention from the very suggestive main evidence Velikovsky had put forward about Venus. And this evidence was not merely mythical or literary, as critics sometimes charged. It drew from geology, planetary science, archaeology, linguistics, iconography, and calendrics.[5] Even in regard to myths, opponents tended to be dismissive, by refusing to consider them, by failing to interpret them correctly, or by pretending not to see the clear meaning of easy-to-interpret myths.

It is worth our while to dwell on the subject of objections because it explains why many scientists thoroughly rejected Velikovsky and it shows how debates like this work. The objections were mostly on scientific grounds, and not all of them were as easy to respond to as the one about global flooding. We might never know, for instance, exactly how the orbit of Venus shifted from being highly elliptical to nearly circular form within a few thousand years. At best we can suggest a half-dozen possible ways and point to other instances of circularized orbits (Chapter 2). But that doesn't mean that rapid circularization was "against the laws of physics"—just that we don't know exactly how it occurred.

Another favorite piece of negative evidence was that Greenland ice cores show no sign of dust and ash from global catastrophes, so none had

---

[5] Reliance on a variety of sources, e.g., calendrics, is considered by some to be the most persuasive criterion for acceptance of a theory (see Chapter 17). Velikovsky's chapter on calendrics in *Worlds in Collision* is factual and well-argued. Most critics steered clear of it.

occurred. In hindsight, we can see that the catastrophes were regionalized along a track of Venus during an approach to Earth, as with the track of a solar eclipse. So they would be widespread but not necessarily global. Also, the relevant dates of ice core and other such evidence need to be revisited in light of more recent findings regarding the timing of the approaches of Venus.

These objections tended to stand each by itself and thus they ran into the problem that Arthur Conan Doyle identified in our prefatory quotation:

> [W]hen a *fact* appears to be opposed to a long train of *deductions*, it *invariably* proves to be capable of bearing some *other interpretation*.[6]

We might wish to change "a long train of *deductions*" to "an array of logically connected evidence", but Conan Doyle's point is clear. Isolated objections, no matter how impressive they may seem to the objector, cannot compete with an array of evidence and logic.

Still, some of the scientific objections to Velikovsky's ideas were right on target.[7] We need not accept even such major ideas of Velikovsky as his revised chronology because the standard chronology makes sense of so many aspects of ancient history, including the dating of Venus sites such as Stonehenge. In addition, he adduced no compelling reasons to think that electromagnetic forces, though no doubt present, play a greater role than gravity in interplanetary interactions. But even in such instances, critics should have asked themselves: Well, we have shown to our satisfaction that Velikovsky was wrong about how X happened, but might X have happened in a different way? As a scientific pathbreaker, Velikovsky had the right to make a pioneer's mistakes as long as he was guiding us in a potentially fruitful direction and providing value along the way. His denigrators should also have considered the potential loss for

---

[6] Arthur Conan Doyle, *A Study in Scarlet* (London: Ward, Lock & Co, 1887)

[7] Critics also found fault with his scholarship, including one instance in which he added to a translation a concocted phrase that made his point: Michael D. Gordin, *The Pseudoscience Wars: Immanuel Velikovsky and the Birth of the Modern Fringe* (Chicago: University of Chicago Press, 2012), 75-77

science and harm to their own reputations if they failed to discern the value in what he offered.

Meanwhile, the critics' objections to Velikovsky's Venus and Reversing Earth theories, arguably his two greatest contributions, seem much less persuasive than the evidence and logic in favor of them. I will present eight new reasons to favor these theories in the Conclusion to this book, when the Reader has more background with which to assess them.

Not surprisingly, however, the scientists who posed those objections to the Venus and Reversing Earth theories considered them as scientifically valid as their objections to other aspects of Velikovsky's portfolio. This led them to think of themselves as defending the laws of science against a charlatan. They used the term pseudoscience to stigmatize Velikovsky and his contributions, a way of ending arguments rather than seeking a better explanation. They were determined to rule out anything he had to say because he represented to them all the forces hostile to science.

Key Pieces

Meanwhile, both Velikovsky and his critics were unaware of key pieces of the puzzle that could have helped resolve the dispute. In the ensuing decades we have found and interpreted new myths that speak with surprising detail about what the ancients saw in the skies. We now know that Venus was widely depicted as an ovoid in ancient iconography, and we know why, permitting us to identify and investigate a wider set of evidence. We now know that the approaches of Venus began shortly before 2500 BC (Velikovsky had thought 1500 BC), in keeping with the standard chronology going back to Manetho's king lists of ancient Egypt. We are aware of the approximate dates of the four inversions: 2200, 1628, 1210, and 820 BC, and they can help us interpret a good deal of other evidence. (Also, if one can identify the approximate dates when something happened, then it's not so easy to deny that it happened!) In turn, we can see that Velikovsky's chronology was just wrong, so that issue no longer needs discussion in regard to the Venus theory.

And very importantly, we now have a superior explanation of the origin of Venus.

Instead of the various unpersuasive suggestions that Velikovsky and others have made for how a cometary Venus could have emerged from Jupiter, we should consider the possible consequences of the immense gravitational field of Jupiter, which pulls into the giant planet a stream of asteroids and comets such as Shoemaker-Levy 9 in 1994. A plausible scenario would have an initially dark, cold proto-Venus, pulled by Jupiter's gravity from the outer solar system shortly before 2500 BC, pass close to Jupiter yet manage to escape its gravitational field. We can term this the Peripheral Passage of Jupiter by Venus, and we can surmise that extreme tidal forces from Jupiter's gravitational field created tremendous heating and a great cometary tail visible to observers on Earth.

This would account for the curious stories of the ancient Greeks, that Athena (Venus—eventually Aphrodite replaced Athena in this role) was born from the head of Zeus (Jupiter), and of the ancient Hindus, that Shukra (Venus) emerged from the mouth of Shiva (Guru or Jupiter). According to Greek myth, Zeus turned the pregnant Metis into a fly who zipped into his mouth. She gave birth to Athena inside of him, and then Athena emerged from his head on the opposite side from his mouth. In effect, a Greek observer spotted proto-Venus when it was approaching Jupiter as tidal friction heated it up to incandescence, and the Greeks called it Metis.

Velikovsky misinterpreted the birth of Athena from the head of Zeus myth to mean that Venus had been explosively expelled from Jupiter itself. His scientific critics rightly considered that bizarre and scientifically unacceptable, so his reputation suffered and his other valuable contributions were rejected.[8]

Proto-Venus would have been large and dense enough to maintain its integrity in the gravitational and magnetic fields of Jupiter even as the entire planet became molten. This Venus would possess a set of elements different from those of Jupiter itself. This scenario would also resolve the

---

[8] Years after hitting upon the idea of an outer solar system origin of Venus, I found that the same idea, minus Metis, had been put forward in 1978 by J.C. Keister and Andrew Hamilton, "An Alternative to the Ejection of Venus from Jupiter in Velikovsky's Catastrophic Theory of the Solar System", *SIS Review*, Vol. III, No. 2 (1978): 45-47. They were evidently ignored.

paradox that Venus is old (the proto-Venus) and yet its surface features appear young (shaped by its Peripheral Passage).

The Peripheral Passage explanation overcomes the three chief objections—escape velocity, elemental composition, and heat generation—to Velikovsky's assertion that Venus emerged as a comet from Jupiter. In turn, this revised explanation of the birth of Venus has led to a generalization of the Venus theory into a theory of the origin of all the terrestrial planets (they were pulled by Jupiter into the inner solar system), for which there is telling evidence. This evidence further buttresses the Venus theory.

The issue of the Jovian origin of Venus has been perhaps the leading criticism of Velikovsky's theories (it was #1 on astronomer Carl Sagan's list) as well as a key reason for denying validity to ancient accounts, many in mythical form, as sources of astronomical, climatic, and geological information. These objections held particular importance because the whole theory depended on the reported emergence of a comet-like Venus from the depths of Jupiter, which seemed outlandish and not credible to critics. Now that this emergence can be seen to have a commonsensical, scientifically plausible explanation, the credibility of the ancient observers, who after all were eyewitnesses, must rise accordingly; and therefore their other stories must be examined more carefully as potential sources of important information. In short, some ancient myths are fanciful; others contain important truths. Refusing to deal with myths is an unpardonable analytical error.

We can see that there is a seamless connection between what planetary and Earth scientists conceive as their subjects and the subject of ancient history. They cannot lay claim to mastery over planetary science and Earth science without first grappling with the relevant aspects of ancient history. Meanwhile, ancient historians need to study up on the relevant planetary science and Earth science, which surely form part of their field.

Two Great Contributions

Meanwhile, new findings and reinterpretations put us into a much better position to assess Velikovsky's real contributions. And speaking in terms of *contributions* is a long-overdue approach in this sobering story of the rejection and vilification of a brilliant scientist. While some of Velikovsky's claims were incorrect and others remain in dispute, we can now speak confidently of two great contributions. The first (with appropriate emendations) is his theory that Venus repeatedly approached Earth during the Bronze Age, causing the BAC, for which there is an array of new evidence and logical deduction on top of what Velikovsky had adduced. The second is his Theory of the Reversing Earth, which has gained added weight from research done after he passed away. These splendid additions to human knowledge not only help us correct many errors but open the door to further additions to what we know.

In effect, part of what Velikovsky argued was right and part was wrong, but the part that was right was far more important.

And what can we say about the critics? They succeeded in identifying much that was wrong with Velikovsky's theories, but they also managed to miss his outstanding contributions. In a classic rush to judgment, they did their best to ruin the reputation of a great scientist and intellectual synthesizer. They also came close to robbing humankind of his fundamental contributions and the opportunities these afforded for reaching other, completely unsuspected, important findings and theories. What's more, researchers in related fields, such as archaeoastronomy and the history of the BAC, have relied on the rejecters, and thus they don't even mention the Venus theory in their own studies, leading to a string of errors. Meanwhile, rejecters and their overly trusting colleagues have been busy teaching these errors to a new generation of students as well as to the public.

So we can shake our heads at the folly of the critics and try our best to learn the lessons of this great case of Scientific Rejectionism.

Of course, before we fully accept all these assertions, we need to examine the evidence and analysis that support them. That is the purpose of the chapters that follow in the first half of this book.

Chapter 2

The Outer Solar System Origin of the Terrestrial Planets

A new theory of the origin of the terrestrial planets—that *Jupiter's gravity pulled them inward from the outer solar system*—solves longstanding scientific riddles and offers a rich agenda for further investigation.

The origin and distribution of water on the terrestrial planets make a good place to start investigating this theory. Radiation pressure and the solar wind pushed water molecules out beyond the "snow line" around 4.5 AU (Astronomical Units, the distance from the Sun to Earth), so how did Earth come to have a relatively significant amount of water?

A common explanation for Earth's oceans—that Earth was bombarded by water-bearing comets—has never been substantiated. The ratio of deuterium to hydrogen in comets is roughly double the ratio in the water on Earth, except for those that formed close to the orbit of Jupiter; but they were short-lived and thus poor candidates. Also, the flux of comets required would be several orders of magnitude larger than appears realistic. Similar considerations hold for asteroids, few of which carry much water. As one researcher states, "the bulk of Earth's water must have been supplied during its formation, rather than steadily throughout geologic time."[9]

New findings regarding the origin of Venus provide a better explanation of why Earth has so much water.

New evidence (see Chapter 1) supports a commonsensical explanation of ancient myths that Venus emerged from Zeus/Jupiter—that Venus was actually pulled from the outer solar system by the gravity of Jupiter and passed near the gas giant, thereby heating up from the tidal force caused by Jupiter's immense gravitational field, losing its ice, gaining a comet tail, and being steered into the inner solar system. All this seems to have happened shortly before 2500 B.C. when the ancients first began to depict Venus as a comet.

Jupiter's Pull

In the early years of the solar system, Jupiter's gravitational field is generally thought to have directed many planetesimals into orbits on the fringes of the solar system, and also some into the inner solar system. So we can posit that all the terrestrial planets were orbiting outside of Jupiter

---

[9] J. Kelly Beatty, Carolyn Collins Petersen, and Andrew Charkin, *The New Solar System*, 4th ed. (Cambridge MA: Cambridge University Press, 1999), 183; A. Morbidelli *et al.*, "Source regions and timescales for the delivery of water to the Earth," *Meteoritics & Planetary Science* 35 (2000): 1309-1320. Largish ice formations in shadowed polar craters on Mercury are also ascribed to cometary or asteroidal impacts 18-53 million years ago but could better be explained by upwelling of aboriginal deep water in response to the shock of otherwise dry impacts. David J. Lawrence *et al.* "Evidence for Water Ice Near Mercury's North Pole from MESSENGER Neutron Spectrometer Measurements," *Sciencexpress*/ http://www.sciencemag.org/content/early/recent/29 November 2012. D/H ratios in the deep mantles of Earth and Mars suggest a primordial origin. Lydia J. Hallis *et al.*, "Evidence for primordial water in Earth's deep mantle," *Science*, Vol. 350, Issue 6262 (2015): 795-7. Localized adsorption of water to dust has also been proposed: Michael J. Drake, "Origin of water in the terrestrial planets," *Meteoritics & Planetary Science*, 40 (2005), Nr 4. But this solution does not account for the wide range of outcomes in the various terrestrial planets.

and then (with the exception of Venus) were pulled by Jupiter into the inner solar system billions of years ago.[10]

Rapid accretion in the early solar system permitted Earth quickly to attain a high mass by impacts with planetesimals. Meanwhile, we know that the regions around the outer planets are exceptionally clear of debris, suggesting that it was all swept up long ago by Saturn, Uranus, and Neptune. But there is one exception.

The slot between Saturn and Uranus appears to contain zones where planetesimals could have orbited without being vacuumed up into these large planets. However, this area is also clear of debris. One explanation is that this was the slot of Venus, which cleaned up these objects until, shortly before 2500 BC, Saturn's gravitational pull or some other cause steered it in the direction of Jupiter, which directed it into the inner solar system.

Various features of Venus—that its surface is so hot, that it appears old yet has a new surface, that it contains 150 times as much deuterium relative to hydrogen compared to Earth (a sign of a large amount of water in the past), that it seems to have a residual tail (the famous but dwindling Black Drop), and that it rotates very slowly in a retrograde direction as if after tidal locking to Jupiter—match the explanation that it passed near Jupiter into the inner solar system. In ancient iconography, Venus was depicted as ovoid, consistent with being stretched by Jupiter's gravity.

Circularization of Orbits

All four terrestrial planets, and the Earth's Moon as well, presumably had highly eccentric orbits when they first entered the inner solar system. Curiously, Mercury (21% eccentricity) and Mars (9%; varies from 0 to 14%) still possess the most eccentric orbits of the eight planets, but Earth

---

[10] The idea that Earth originated in the outer solar system, thereby accounting for its water, has been suggested by various researchers. In the early twentieth century Thomas Jefferson Jackson See argued that the Moon had come from the outer solar system, perhaps pulled by Jupiter's gravity.

(<2%) and Venus (<1%) have very circular ones. The requirement for a speedy circularization of the orbit of Venus has been a major focus of critics of the ancient evidence that suggests that it entered the inner solar system shortly before 2500 BC.

What properties do Earth and Venus share that led their orbits to become circular?

First, the Earth has oceans, and both planets have thick atmospheres, that created the plasticity that reduced the eccentricity of their orbits.[11] Second, both were very hot in their early years in the inner solar system. This heat made them more plastic and thus more pliant to the gravitational pull of the Sun, which tended to render their orbits more circular. Third, the giant cometary tail of Venus and the Earth's Moon in parallel fashion tended to lessen the eccentricity. Fourth, Earth and Venus both interacted with other planets in ways that made their orbits more circular. Specifically, each of more than 30 passages of Venus near Earth every 52 years between ~2525 BC and ~700 BC, via gravitational tugging, bent Venus' orbit and made it ever more circular. Fifth, in ancient times Venus had a markedly ovoid shape. Comet Venus appears to have moved at times in the direction of its major axis, and this added to its length and malleability under gravitational forces and thereby its tendency to circularize its orbit. Having lost Mars (see below), Earth, too, initially had a less-than-uniformly spherical shape and thus might have been less resistant to circularization of orbit. Sixth, the electromagnetic force might have played a role, though in what manner and to what extent need to be modeled, including whether the tails formed dusty plasmas with electric and magnetic properties.

In fact, scientists generally recognize that rapid circularization must occur in the presumably originally highly elliptical orbits of short-term comets that end up with circular orbits, otherwise they would lose their material when interacting closely with the Sun on hundreds or thousands

---

[11] Chris Sherrerd, "Venus' Circular Orbit," *Pensée,* Vol. 2, No 2 (May 1972): 43

of highly elliptical passes. Comet Venus evidently resembled such comets.[12]

A discussion of the orbits of planetesimals concludes: "Most close encounters between planetesimals did not lead to a collision, but bodies often pass close enough for their mutual gravitational tug to change their orbits. Statistical studies show that after many such close encounters, high-mass bodies tend to acquire circular, coplanar orbits."[13]

Comet Moon

In keeping with the Outer Solar System Origin of the Terrestrial Planets (OSSO), one can see a solution to the puzzle of the origin of the Earth-Moon system that makes sense of the capture theory, often thought implausible because of tight parameters of velocity, starting position, and chemistry that the Moon would need to fulfill. Of course, the various satellites in retrograde orbit around the outer planets suggest that capture is not so improbable after all.

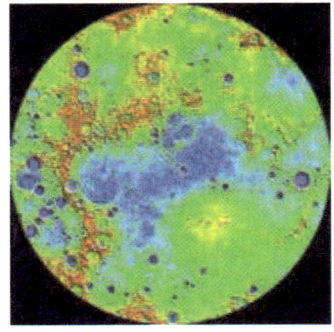

Figure 2. North Pole of Mercury

Initially, a smallish protoplanet ("Merculuna"), which had come from an orbit close to the original orbit of Earth outside of Jupiter (to make sense of the close match between the oxygen ratios of Earth and Moon), heated up tremendously on its passage past the gas giant. The force exerted by Jupiter's gravity pulled a small molten part out of the larger part. The larger part, containing the main iron core, continued on into the inner solar system as Mercury. Its magnetic field was shifted roughly 20% of its radius to the north of its equator, suggesting that

---

[12] M.E. Bailey, S.V.M. Clube, and W.M. Napier, *The Origin of Comets* (Oxford: Pergamon, 1989) 155 ff; Charles Ginenthal, *Carl Sagan & Immanuel Velikovsky* (Tempe AZ: Falcon, 1995), 404.

[13] Tilman Spohn, Doris Breuer, and Torrence Johnson, eds., *Encyclopedia of the Solar System*, 3rd edition, (Amsterdam: Elsevier, 2014), 43

Mercury had lost a major component (the Moon) from its north pole (this NASA image of Mercury's northern hemisphere shows a depressed darker polar region). A highly reflective area in a several-kilometer deep depression at the pole strongly suggests water ice—and this water ice, as we saw above, is in all likelihood aboriginal, too much to be conveyed by comets. Mercury's south pole correspondingly has a small depressed area at its center surrounded by what appear to be faint concentric rings, consistent with an area of antipodal disruption that had been sucked inward as the Moon was pulling free from the north pole region.

The other piece of Merculuna, composed of a small amount of iron[14] but mainly of silicate rock, with most of the volatiles in its crust and upper mantle, including water, burned away by the heat, and with a long comet tail of rock and dust shed from its surface, also escaped Jupiter and proceeded into the inner solar system. This partly molten Comet Moon was malleable and prone to entanglement with the gravitational field of Earth. Its separation from Mercury left it skewed both in shape and in elemental distribution. The giant Oceanus Procellarum on the near side is the scar left by the separation event. The rectangular shape of the gravity anomaly surrounding it sharply distinguishes it from impact craters. Consistent with this, the evidence of higher heating found on the surface and upper mantle of the near side can be interpreted as the consequence of the near side having been the highest energy intensity location as the Moon was torn from Mercury during the separation event. The unusually high magnetic field around the Reiner Gamma Formation within the Oceanus Procellarum fits this picture.

Figure 3. Oceanus Procellarum

---

[14] And yet bearing geochemical evidence that "a large amount of metallic iron was once in contact with the substance of the Moon", i.e., the high iron content that remained with Mercury: John A. Wood, "Moon Over Mauna Loa: A Review of Hypotheses of Formation of Earth's Moon" in W. Hartmann, ed., *Origin of the Moon* (Houston: Lunar and Planetary Institute, 1986), 39-40.

Once separated from Mercury, Moon followed closely the trajectory of Earth and ended up in approximately the same orbital slot as Earth. Thus Moon shared with Earth a similar niche of origin, a similar trajectory, roughly matching chemistry, and presumably a roughly similar velocity. The tight parameters of the old capture theory gave way to generous parameters within which Comet Moon—exceedingly responsive to tidal forces—readily fit; and, perhaps after a number of misses, it ended up orbiting the Earth in an initially highly eccentric but gradually circularizing orbit, slowly cooling and losing its comet tail yet retaining the memory of its heated state in a rather small molten outer core and an extremely hot, dense, solid inner core.[15] (Mercury possesses a molten core.[16]) This scenario of a Moon with a highly eccentric orbit upon capture provides a nice match with data regarding the Moon's three principal moments of inertia, which are not consistent with the Giant Impact theory.[17] It also suggests that many of the solar system's moons were captured comets.

The finding that lunar melt inclusions protected by crystals contain fairly high levels of water as well as other volatiles[18] seems consistent with this scenario of high, steady heat that caused the outgassing of almost all

---

[15] http://news.sciencemag.org/sciencenow/2011/01/at-long-last-moons-core-seen.html?ref=hp. The concept of a hot, deformable Moon (but without a cometary origin or tail) can be found in R.R. Winters and R.J. Malcuit, "The Lunar Capture Hypothesis Revisited," *The Moon* 17 (1977): 353-8. The authors calculate that reasonable parameters would permit about one-fourth of the energy of deformation to be dissipated, thus permitting capture of the Moon by the Earth. The addition of a comet tail would reinforce this conclusion. In other words, the capture of Comet Moon has been (approximately) mathematically modeled. See also an estimate that the increase of temperature from dissipation of energy connected with the initial highly eccentric orbit of a captured Moon inside the Moon itself would have been 2-5000°C. This would have contributed to the very high heat of the core: Horst Gerstenkorn, "The earliest past of the Earth-Moon system," *Icarus*, 11 (1969): 189-207, p. 197.
[16] J.L. Margot *et al.*, "Large Longitude Libration of Mercury Reveals a Molten Core," *Science* 316, 4 May 2007: 10-14
[17] Ian Garrick-Bethell, Jack Wisdom, Maria T. Zuber, "Evidence for a Past High-Eccentricity Lunar Orbit," *Science* 313, 4 August 2006: 652-5
[18] E.H. Hauri *et al.*, "High Pre-Eruptive Water Contents Preserved in Lunar Melt Inclusions," www.sciencexpress.org / 26 May 2011 / 10.1125/science.1204626

volatiles down to 500 km depth except those in the crystals, whereas it seems very inconsistent with the Giant Impact hypothesis of the origin of the Moon, which entails an ultra-high energy event that would presumably have melted the crystals. As the authors of the lunar melt inclusion article note, their evidence rules out the arrival of water after the heating that the crystals withstood; the water was preexisting—a good match with an origin in an icy Merculuna in the outer solar system.

In effect, Comet Moon was hot enough to lose surface matter that then formed a tail, to outgas almost all volatiles down to 500 km, and to be sufficiently malleable that the Earth's gravitational field could capture it; but not so hot as to destroy the crystals that encapsulated volatiles or completely to smooth over the indented surface where the near side had been torn from Mercury. Moon's top 500 km thus were tidally heated to a high degree during the peripheral passage of Jupiter, then cooled, while the core remained exceptionally hot as a memento of the high-energy separation from Mercury.

The theory also provides explanations of Mercury's molten core; relatively high orbital eccentricity; very high iron content; and skewed distribution of magnetic field so that the northern hemisphere has a higher magnetic field, consistent with a separation event in which Jupiter's gravitational field pulled material from its north pole region. Instead of two *ad hoc* giant impacts with complicated post-impact scenarios, a single separation event integral to OSSO during the peripheral passage of Jupiter accounts for the distinctive features of the Moon and Mercury.

Because Mercury has 4.5 times the mass of the Moon, it was more resistant to heating up during the peripheral passage of Jupiter than the Moon was. Mercury also was more resistant to Jupiter's gravitational pull after separation and so might have followed a slightly more distant trajectory from Jupiter. The consequently relatively lower temperature could explain why Mercury has much higher levels of potassium and sulfur, which were lost by the hot Comet Moon. Data from the MESSENGER orbiter are very consistent with a Mercury-Moon separation event, whereas they undermine competing hypotheses such as a giant impact that caused Mercury to lose a putative original thick coating of silicate rock.[19]

The Moon possesses remanent high-intensity paleomagnetism seemingly derived from a dynamo; and its intensity surpasses the capacity of the small lunar core to generate a field.[20] These characteristics are plausibly the consequences of a Merculuna dynamo that the Moon lost upon separation, possibly about 3.92 billion years ago (it is not clear, however, how the Moon's magnetic field remained at a high level for many millions of years thereafter, suggesting that an unsuspected mechanism generated the field). Until about perhaps 3.85 billion years ago, both the Moon and Mercury, on highly elliptical orbits, passed repeatedly through the asteroid belt, accounting for their similarly heavily cratered surfaces and obviating the need for the Late Heavy Bombardment hypothesis. Then, before the Moon cooled and lost plasticity as well as perhaps its comet tail, it was captured by Earth. This dating contradicts the Giant Impact hypothesis of the Moon's origin, which places that putative event many hundreds of millions of years earlier. Supporting this interpretation is evidence from zircons that Earth's surface temperature from 4.4 billion years ago was under 200°C, which the authors take to mean that any Giant Impact must have happened before then; but they question whether there was such a putative Giant Impact and note that a capture of the Moon would not have affected Earth's surface temperature.[21]

This explanation of the origin of the Moon also provides a solution to the lunar inclination problem: the high obliquity of the Moon's orbit (5.1°) is in the vicinity of the obliquity of Mercury's orbit (7.0°), and it is higher than the obliquities of the orbits of the other planets.

---

[19] Richard A. Kerr, "Mercury Looking Less Exotic, More a Member of the Family," *Science*, Vol. 333, 30 September 2011: 1812 and the detailed articles in the same issue.
[20] B.P. Weiss and S.M. Tikoo, "The lunar dynamo," *Science*, Vol. 346, 5 December 2014, DOI:10.1126/science.1246753
[21] John W. Valley *et al.*, "A cool early Earth," *Geology*, Vol. 30, 2002: 351-4

Comets Earth and Mars

According to OSSO, Jupiter's gravitational field also pulled the Earth into the inner solar system. Tidal heating caused by passing Jupiter accounts for evidence that the Earth's surface once had a magma ocean, and shedding of surface materials and loss of a primitive atmosphere created a cometary tail. As with Moon and Mercury, it appears that Mars and the Earth originally formed a single protoplanet ("Terramars"), and the immense gravitational field of Jupiter pulled Mars out of the Earth (forming the Pacific Basin) as the protoplanet passed by.

Here are reasons to think that this is in fact correct: 1) Mars resembled Earth in originally having a great deal of water; 2) the higher density of the Earth is consistent with a larger body from which the smaller, less dense Mars was extracted in a separation event, analogous to Mercury and the Moon; 3) the 9.5:1 ratio of mass between Earth and Mars is likewise consistent with such an extraction; 4) the diameter of Mars, 6792 km, is roughly consistent with the distance across the Pacific between San Francisco and Tokyo, 8266 km; 5) Mars' north pole is surrounded by circular scarring, suggesting that it was the last part of Mars attached to Earth's Pacific Basin as Terramars was torn apart by Jupiter's gravity; 6) circular scarring also surrounds the south pole of Mars, suggestive of antipodal disruption, as in Mercury's south pole; and 7) the sharp difference between the northern and southern hemispheres of Mars arose from a separation event that left the northern hemisphere crust thin and vulnerable to subsequent remodeling by flood basalts provoked by other causes, though a later giant impact[22] also played a major role in shaping the northern hemisphere. The extreme extent of the Borealis planitia, its irregular, non-elliptical shape, and the 2-3 km scarp that surrounds it are signs of such a pre-impact birth scar from a separation event, fittingly all on the opposite side of the planet from the tidal bulge of the southern highlands, which is not accounted for by the giant impact alone.

---

[22] Jeffrey C. Andrews-Hanna, Maria T. Zuber, W. Bruce Banerdt, "The Borealis basin and the origin of the martian crustal dichotomy," *Nature* 453, 26 June 2008: 1212-15

The remanent magnetization in banded stripes of alternating polarity in Mars' southern hemisphere is reminiscent of the magnetization of the spreading zones beneath the Earth's oceans. It results from a powerful, dynamo-driven alternating dipole magnetic field and represents an outstanding anomaly in a Mars that lacks a dynamo and has only a tiny, non-dipole magnetic field. In the context of OSSO, however, this magnetization can be interpreted as having been formed by the original magnetic field of Terramars.

The catastrophic separation while passing Jupiter and the interaction with the giant planet's immense gravitational and magnetic fields diminished the dynamo in Earth while ending any dynamo in Mars. In turn, this suggests that Earth's plate tectonics and geomagnetic field go back to Terramars. Since weathering and plate tectonics have destroyed any evidence of the original surface of the Earth, Mars' southern hemisphere, though heavily bombarded, comprises the only remaining original surface of Terramars. In contrast to Mercury and the Moon, the bombardment of the southern hemisphere of Mars began at the time it was separated from Earth, approximately 4.5 billion years ago. Mars appears to have maintained an elliptical orbit that carried it repeatedly through the asteroid belt until perhaps 3.8-3.7 billion years ago, accounting for the heavy cratering in its southern hemisphere and the late formation of the Hellas Basin. As with Mercury and the Moon, this renders unnecessary the Late Heavy Bombardment hypothesis. Then Mars' orbit became less elliptical than before.

All of these phenomena are evidence of a tectonic regime that is very much what we might expect of the location of the emergence of Mars.

In an early version of the old, generally discredited fission theory of the origin of the Earth-Moon system, the Pacific Basin was a scar left over from the separation of the Moon from a rapidly rotating Earth. But according to OSSO, the center of the geomagnetic field, roughly modeled as if a bar magnet dipole were buried inside the Earth, is displaced 498 km off Earth's center of figure in the direction of the Pacific Basin at 25° N, 153° E because Mars was separated from Earth there as Terramars passed Jupiter. Not only the skew of the geomagnetic field but also the Pacific Basin itself and the Hawaiian and South Pacific hotspots are physical leftovers from the separation of Mars from Earth. Much evidence supports this, including the Ring of Fire of seismic and volcanic activity approximately surrounding the crudely circular Pacific and the thinner (by 2 km) crust of the Pacific compared to the Atlantic crust.

Another leftover of the separation at the Pacific Basin is the South Atlantic Magnetic Anomaly on the opposite side of the world whereby the Van Allen radiation belt comes close to Earth as a consequence of the skew in the geomagnetic field. Arguably, the antipodal disruption caused by the emergence of Mars from the North Pacific also contributed to Africa's rich deposits of exotic minerals.

Thus the large low shear-wave velocity provinces beneath the Pacific (Jason) and Africa (Tuzo) were formed by the emergence of Mars. This knowledge enables paleogeographers to track proto-continents and True Polar Wander farther back in time than previously.

Given the long, tangled history of plate tectonics, continental drift, and other intervening phenomena, the present-day Pacific Basin has changed considerably since its origin in the primeval Panthalassic Ocean, itself a descendant of the original Mirovia Ocean. Still, seismic anisotropy reveals a unique pancake-like pattern at 160 km depth, approximately centered on the island of Hawaii,[23] though Mars' emergence was not

---

[23] C. Gaboret, A.M. Forte, J.-P. Montager, "The unique dynamics of the Pacific Hemisphere mantle and its signature on seismic anisotropy," *Earth and Planetary Science Letters* 208 (2003): 219-33. See especially Figure 4, p. 227. In similar fashion, an anomalous annulus of higher seismic velocities indicative of colder rock at 2770 km depth in the core-mantle boundary region surrounds the Pacific: Lisa Tauxe, *Essentials of Paleomagnetism* (Berkeley: University of California, 2010): 267-8; see also image #c of Figure 14.11, p. 281; the original, more detailed graphics are in G. Masters *et al.*, "The Relative Behavior of Shear Velocity, Bulk Sound Speed, and Compressional Velocity in the Mantle: Implications for Chemical and Thermal Structure" in S. Karato *et al.*, eds., *Earth's Deep Interior*, Vol. 117 (2000) of AGU Monograph (Washington, D.C.: American Geophysical Union, 2000): 63-87, with the graphics at 2770 km depth on pp. 77 and 78. In general, the geology of the Pacific Basin contains a number of features consistent with an emergence of Mars. In a list of hotspot/melting anomaly locations, for instance, Pacific plate hotspots score consistently much higher in terms of flow rate than Atlantic and Indian Ocean counterparts, and they are matched only by several at the near edges of the adjacent Nazca and Australian plates: G.R. Foulger and D.M. Jurdy, eds., *Plates, Plumes, and Planetary Processes* (Boulder CO: Geological Society of America,

necessarily centered on the Hawaiian hotspot, and it seems to have left an oval wound, a kind of peeling off, extending into the South Pacific with its hotspots and anomalies.

The emergence of Mars was also the origin of the distinction between the oceanic and continental hemispheres discussed by Peter Warlow[24] and divided by a secondary equator that served as an alternative to the standard equator in some episodes of True Polar Wander and inversions.

The immense heat generated by the Earth's peripheral passage of Jupiter was stored throughout its mass. This could explain why the Earth's surface remained warm enough for water during its early years even though the Sun shone at only about 70% of its present output (the Faint Young Sun Paradox).

When did Terramars separate into Earth and Mars? Proponents of the Giant Impact theory of the formation of the Moon have found evidence that various asteroids were all struck by fragments that appear to have come from a great cataclysm around 105 million years after the beginning of the solar system 4.6 billion years ago.[25] They consider this cataclysm to be their Giant Impact, but according to OSSO that never occurred. Instead, it seems very possible that these fragments came from the separation of Earth from Mars, and so they provide a candidate date for this event.

A separation of Earth and Mars would reduce the number of Peripheral Passages of Jupiter, thus in a sense simplifying the entire OSSO theory. In two cases (Merculuna and Terramars), a separation event occurred. In the third one (Venus), the pull of Jupiter's gravity caused an elongation of the planet into an ovoid shape, as depicted in ancient iconography, suggesting that Venus, too, had been very close to experiencing its own separation event while passing Jupiter—i.e., that stretching to the point of separation

---

2007), 65-78, replicated in G.R. Foulger, *Plates vs Plumes: A Geological Controversy* (Oxford: Wiley-Blackwell, 2010), 15-6. The 1-km high Hawaiian swell and the 500-m high South Pacific Superswell also mark the Pacific Basin as idiosyncratic.

[24] Peter Warlow, *The Reversing Earth* (London: J.M. Dent & Sons, 1982)

[25] *Science*, 17 April 2015, Vol. 348 Issue 6232: 271 and especially W.F. Bottke *et al.*, "Dating the Moon-forming Impact Event with Asteroidal Meteorites," 321-323

was a normal process during a Peripheral Passage of Jupiter. Just three instances in 4.5 billion years help overcome the objection that it was very unlikely that Jupiter would throw the planets into exactly the right direction to enter the inner solar system (without hitting the Sun) instead of dispatching them to the far reaches of the solar system or beyond it. These were appropriately rare events.

While each of the terrestrial planets underwent unique experiences following the Peripheral Passage of Jupiter, in terms of axial tilt Mercury (0.01°) is closest to the Moon (1.54°) and the axial tilt of Earth (23.4°) is closest to that of Mars (25.19°). In terms of orbital inclination to the ecliptic, again Mercury (7.01°) and the Moon (5.145°) form a fairly close match, as do Earth (0°) and Mars (1.85°). In general, OSSO provides a simple explanation of the obliquities and orbital inclinations of the terrestrial planets, in contrast to the theory of *in situ* formation, which requires *ad hoc* collisions with large objects as accretion came to a close.

Lopsided

Thus we can explain the remarkable, anomalous lopsidedness of the terrestrial planets as a consequence of Jupiter's gravitational pull during Peripheral Passages. The southern hemisphere of Mars and the far side of the Moon are both tidal bulges that were pulled out by Jupiter's gravitational field. On Mars the northern hemisphere crust is 35 km thick, while the southern highlands crust is 80 km. On the Moon, the near side crust is 60 km thick, while the far side crust is on average up to 100 km thick if the thin crust, resulting from an impact, under the South Pole-Aitken Basin is excluded. The center of mass of Mars is displaced 3.5 km to the north from the center of figure, while the center of mass of the Moon is displaced 1.68 km +/-50 m to the nearside from the center of figure. Meanwhile, Mercury has considerably more iron in its northern hemisphere than in the south, while both the Earth's inner core and its center of mass (2.1 km from the center of figure) are asymmetrical. In both cases of separation, the lighter molten rock would have more readily been pulled by Jupiter's gravity into the tidal bulges.

We can expect that the larger partner planet emerging from the separation would have a higher density, being more resistant to the tidal force from Jupiter than the smaller one; and this is indeed the case: the uncompressed density of Mercury is 5.3 grams per cm^3 while that of the Moon is 3.3, and the density of the Earth is 4.4 while that of Mars is 3.7. Venus has an uncompressed density of 4.3, which is in line with that of the Earth; and the density of Venus is situated between the densities of Mercury and the Moon.[26]

In other words, crustal thickness, displacement of center of mass, and uncompressed density of the terrestrial planets all are consistent with being the consequences of a Peripheral Passage of Jupiter.

One can predict that a similar distribution of elements, from light to heavy across the planet, will be found on Venus. Tidal locking, as noted above, caused the anomalous very slow, retrograde rotation of Venus as well as the discrepancy between its center of figure and its center of mass. At 0.28 km, this distance is smaller than those of the other terrestrial planets, but it is much larger than expected error. It seems logical that the stretching of Venus during partial tidal locking would leave a distinguishable yet less prominent lopsidedness than in the planets that were torn in two. Meanwhile, Venus' perfectly spheroidal shape, evidently the result of remodeling since its pronounced ovoid appearance in ancient iconography, also makes it an outlier: there is no sign of oblateness.

In contrast to the other two Peripheral Passages of Jupiter in OSSO, the Peripheral Passage of Venus just before 2500 BC was observed by at least one Greek eyewitness and was recorded in the easy-to-interpret myths of Metis and the birth of Athena. Although Immanuel Velikovsky incorrectly assumed that Venus had emerged from Jupiter itself and that it had approached Earth around 1500 BC, his account of the subsequent interactions of Comet Venus with Earth contains a great deal of evidence regarding the later stages of an OSSO event as observed by human eyewitnesses.

---

[26] de Pater and Lissauer, 242

Conclusion

OSSO must lead us to revise current views on:

1. the importance of impacts. They clearly played a significant role but not so dominant a one as has been supposed. Close encounters have shaped the inner solar system in fundamental ways;
2. the presence of dust and gas in the early inner solar system. While larger dust particles spiraled into the Sun from Poynting-Robertson drag and other kinds of drag, radiation pressure and the solar wind rapidly pushed tiny particles and gas out to or beyond the asteroid belt or beyond the "snow line" (4.5 AU). There was no need for very rapid accretion of the terrestrial planets before the inner solar system was cleared of dust and gas[27] because they formed in the outer solar system. Nor, for the same reason, are the low mass of Mars and the main asteroid belt anomalous compared to the mass of Venus and Earth.[28] Meanwhile, evidence for the finding that asteroids of the CL chondrite class were the source of Earth's volatiles can be reinterpreted to mean that CL chondrites and Earth originated in the same region of the solar system.[29] In effect, the area roughly between the present-day orbits of Jupiter and Saturn was the birthplace of the planets, from which some of them wandered outward from the Sun while others were pulled inward;
3. the origin of water on the terrestrial planets. OSSO provides a simple explanation;
4. the hypothetical Late Heavy Bombardment, which never happened;

---

[27] Ibid., 530, 534
[28] Ibid., 542-3
[29] C.M.O'D. Alexander *et al.*, "The Provenances of Asteroids, and Their Contributions to the Volatile Inventories of the Terrestrial Planets," *Science,* Vol. 337, 10 August 2012: 721-723. See also Paul Voosen. Meteorite divide points to solar system chaos. *Science*. Vol. 359, 30 March 2018: 1451.

5. the Giant Impact hypothesis of the formation of the Earth-Moon system, which is incorrect. OSSO provides superior explanations of the Moon's heavily cratered surface, the near side/far side dichotomy (including surface features and crustal depths), the complementary low iron of the Moon and high iron of Mercury, the lunar magnetic field, Oceanus Procellarum, lunar melt inclusions, the displacement of the center of mass of the Moon, and thermal layering. All of these are integral features of OSSO, so the evidence and arguments on other topics in OSSO support them, unlike with the *ad hoc* evidence and arguments in the models of the Giant Impact hypothesis;
6. the origin of the Pacific Basin, the seismic anomalies beneath it, and the Ring of Fire that surrounds it;
7. key features of Mercury;
8. Mars, once part of our planet; and
9. Venus. OSSO offers telling evidence and explanations that make more believable the mythical accounts of the ancients and, following them and much other evidence, the interpretation of Immanuel Velikovsky that Venus emerged from (in fact, passed close to) Jupiter and entered the inner solar system during the Bronze Age. It provides simple, parsimonious, appropriate solutions to otherwise poorly explained anomalies of Venus.

The OSSO theory possesses significant marks of superiority compared to other explanations. Above all, it powerfully explains two outstanding anomalies: the origin and features of the Pacific Basin, and the otherwise inexplicable array of new evidence regarding the origin and approaches of Venus during the Bronze Age.

Chapter 3

The Martian Theory of Mass Extinctions

There is no shortage of candidates for the cause of the mass extinctions of prehistory. But experts have found flaws in every one.

Asteroid impact at Chicxulub, Yucatan clearly played a role in the Cretaceous-Tertiary (KT) extinction that wiped out the dinosaurs (except birds) 65,000,000 years ago, though scientists point to the serious disruptions that had begun hundreds of thousands of years before with the basalt flows of the Deccan Traps.[30] Giant basalt lava flows that poisoned the atmosphere and oceans played a role in four, or perhaps all five, major extinctions. But other enormous basalt flows have not caused extinctions, nor did they cause the tsunamis associated with various extinctions.[31]

---

[30] According to the authors of a study of global lithium isotope distribution around 65 million years ago, neither the Chicxulub impact nor the Deccan Traps had the capacity to account for the extreme, worldwide weathering of rocks and denudation of land surfaces: Sambuddha Misra and Philip N. Froelich, "Lithium Isotope History of Cenozoic Seawater: Changes in Silicate Weathering and Reverse Weathering," *Science* 335, 17 February 2012: 818-23. The boundary is also termed the Cretaceous-Paleogene (K-Pg).

[31] Du, Yuansheng *et al.*, "Devonian Frasnian-Famennian transitional event deposits of Guangxi, South China and their possible tsunami origin," *Science in China Series D: Earth Sciences*, Nov. 2008, 51/11: 1570-1580

Researchers have suggested many other mechanisms, but there's no consensus at all.

Lurking in the background, however, is a quite plausible cause, one that would have possessed the power to set off the volcanic activity, sea level shifts, loss of oxygen in oceans, climate changes, and other phenomena associated with the extinctions.

The Martian Theory

The new candidate is the Martian Theory of Mass Extinctions (MTME). According to MTME, repeated approaches by Mars to Earth at irregular intervals caused tidal movements in already stressed geological formations, setting off widespread volcanic eruptions and activating mantle heating and plumes that led to hundreds of thousands of years of gargantuan lava flows. Mountainous tsunamis and earthquakes added to the destruction.

According to MTME, the orbits of Earth and Mars intersected at their extremities, in particular during the period from 600,000,000 to 65,000,000 years ago. At random intervals, the two planets had close encounters, triggering mass extinctions on Earth and parallel massive geological activity on Mars (gigantic volcanoes and the extensive uplifted Tharsis region—over 4 billion years old). It seems plausible that the same gravitational force of Earth that lifted the Tharsis region caused the giant rift of the nearby Valles Marineris, though exactly how is not clear. In other words, MTME would account for several of the outstanding features of the surface of Mars as well as lesser ones like perched craters and the tall cliff surrounding Olympus Mons. Roughly speaking, the closer the encounter, the greater the extinction on Earth and concurrent geological activity on Mars, so MTME could account for minor extinctions as well, though these might have had other causes.

The same gravitational rifting that created the Valles Marineris may also have carved out the original Grand Canyon, its smaller size reflecting the less powerful pull of Mars on the Earth. The *Barrancas del Cobre* valleys of northwest Mexico, usually explained as resulting from volcanic activity 30-40,000,000 years ago, might actually have originated similarly at the same time.

Earlier interactions account for the huge Martian outwash channels (from rapidly melted permafrost and release of water from underground reservoirs) and older volcanoes such as Elysium Mons as well. Earth's approaches may have left the evidence of giant tsunamis on Mars about 3.4 billion years ago.[32] Tectonic activity and weathering on the Earth destroyed much of the evidence of early interactions, but clues on Mars could lead to a reinterpretation of early fossil evidence on Earth of extinctions during the first 2 1/2 billion years of life. Clustered dramatic fluctuations in climate and radical drops in photosynthesis, for instance, are characteristic of Snowball/Slushball Earth episodes and of the five main mass extinctions, so they may share a common Martian approach trigger. Distinct stages in the evolution of Earth systems, including the biological one, could account for the differences between them.

MTME encounters with Mars provide a plausible cause of at least some of the high number of gaps in the stratigraphic record and of some of the overthrusts found worldwide. In theory, as Mars came closest to the Earth, its gravity lifted and pulled stratigraphic layers out of alignment. Repeated approaches of Mars from somewhat different angles caused the patchquilt effect seen around the world, with only a few areas completely spared.

Cyclical approaches of Mars explain one researcher's perception that there could have been "serial extra-terrestrial insults" that kept the extinctions going and cut short attempted recoveries.[33] Finally, perhaps after a particularly close encounter, the path of the smaller Mars (roughly 1/9 the mass of Earth) was altered by the interaction with Earth, and Mars adopted a somewhat different orbit for tens of millions of years. Then mutual gravitational attraction gradually brought the two planets together again.

---

[32] Rodriguez, J. A. P. *et al*. "Tsunami waves extensively resurfaced the shorelines of an early Martian ocean," *Nature Scientific Reports* 6, 25106; doi: 10.1038/srep25106 (2016)

[33] Roger Buick in Peter D. Ward, *Under a Green Sky* (New York: HarperCollins, 2007), 79

Objections to MTME

Objection #1. *In keeping with the Moon's tiny influence on tidal heating of Earth, Mars would not possess the capacity to induce sufficient heating to melt rocks and initiate the lava flows of flood basalts.* But Mars has approximately 9 times the mass of the Moon. Therefore, at the Moon's current distance from the Earth of 384,000 km, Mars would exert 9 times the force of the Moon. At 38,400 km, Mars would exert 9 x 10 = 90 times the force of the Moon. And at 3,840 km, Mars would exert 90 x 10 = 900 times the force of the Moon—more than enough to do the job.

Objection #2. *Even a force hundreds of times the gravitational force of the Moon would not set off a massive flood basalt flow.* In regard to the Earth's lithosphere, some geologists favor the explanation of the flood basalts as triggered by heating and melting of rock in a relatively small zone just outside the edge of a craton and not too deep. The heating and melting then propagate to entrain more rock from beneath the craton to heat up, melt, and flow.[34] Also, the amount of gravitational force (causing tidal heating) exerted by Mars necessary to bring the initial rock up to the melting point would not be large because the gravitational pull would "seek out" the point of vulnerability where the existing temperature of the rock (increasing with depth) plus the added tidal heating (according to a

---

[34]In response to the objection that the gravitational pull of Mars would not have reached far enough into the Earth to entrain tidal heating that would melt massive amounts of rock, see pp. 636-7 of Irina M. Artemieva, *The Lithosphere: An Interdisciplinary Approach* (Cambridge: Cambridge University Press, 2011). She suggests that, in the origin of flood basalts, the deep plume mechanism doesn't fit as well as "edge-driven secondary convection" that affects much shallower rock. She synthesizes a model proposed by Scott D. King and Don L. Anderson, "An alternative mechanism of flood basalt formation," *Earth and Planetary Science Letters* 136 (1995): 269-79 and a 1988 article by Yu. A. Zorin and B.M. Vladimirov, "The Thermal Regime of the Lithosphere of the Siberian Platform and the Problem of the Origin of the Traps," *Izvestiia Akademii Nauk SSR. Seriya Geologicheskaya* 8, 1988: 130-32 (in Russian) that argues that the Siberian Traps contain high-iron eclogites from partial melting of the lower lithosphere (and thus not from a deep mantle source).

gravitational pull gradient diminishing with depth) would first surpass the temperature needed to melt sufficient rock.

Alternatively, Mars' gravitational pull could set off a powerful earthquake that would in turn lead to heating and melting of rock at the point of vulnerability. Direct heating by tidal friction and indirect heating via a seismic intermediary could also have acted together to trigger melting of rock.

Or an approach of Mars could have triggered a response in the fluid, largely iron outer core that, in turn, would cause a mantle plume that would fuel the eruption of flood basalts.

Objection #3. *The force exerted by Earth on Mars at such close quarters would have melted the entire surface of Mars, assuming that Mars came close enough to melt a part of the Earth's lithosphere.* This effect, however, would have been constricted by tidal locking. Either the great volcanoes or the Tharsis bulge would have locked onto Earth during an encounter, and so the greatest force of Earth's gravity would have focused on that point. In turn, the surface of the surrounding area of the northern hemisphere of Mars might indeed have melted, but the locking would have kept the surface of Mars' southern hemisphere intact. As Mars rotated upon approaching Earth, whatever part of Mars' surface would have initially come into closest contact with Earth would have quickly given way to Mars' most vulnerable and prominent locking points—the volcanoes and the Tharsis bulge—so that the southern hemisphere would have never undergone sustained severe direct gravitational pull.

In other words, during a near miss Mars would have possessed a much greater capacity than the Moon to cause tidal heating on Earth yet would have avoided having its entire surface melted by Earth.[35]

---

[35] Cf William James Burroughs, *Climate Change: A Multidisciplinary Approach,* 2nd ed. (New York: Cambridge University Press, 2007), 175: "The direct influence of tides could influence the release of tectonic energy in the form of volcanism. Since there is evidence that major volcanic eruptions have triggered periods of climate cooling, this would enable small extraterrestrial effects to be amplified to produce more significant climatic fluctuations."

Searching for Evidence

How can we test the Martian Theory?

First, comparing the Bronze Age catastrophes and the mass extinctions could shed light on both. For instance, as we will discuss in Chapter 4, there are good reasons to think that during the Bronze Age catastrophes the Earth, under the influence of Venus' gravity, turned over four times, in approximately 2020, 1628, 1210, and 820 BC. Giant tsunamis swept far inland in China and elsewhere. Since Mars exerted a larger gravitational effect during its very close prehistoric encounters, it is likely that the Earth inverted in response, and much more rapidly than the ten-day duration of the Bronze Age inversions, perhaps in a single day, thereby upturning the water column and disrupting circulation patterns. Each rapid prehistoric inversion would have caused tsunamis that dwarfed those of the Bronze Age and would have greatly contributed to the exceptional devastation of the mass extinctions. Evidence of such tsunamis has been mistakenly attributed to bolide impacts.[36] MTME would also explain the evidence for a tsunami in a southern embayment of Argentina[37] better than the Chicxulub impact. Repeated very close approaches of Mars could have caused several inversions in close proximity,[38] while the rapidity and hence the destructiveness of the inversion could have been related to the closeness of approach, which would explain why the largest five mass extinctions differed in extent.

Second, we need to seek much better detail on Martian volcanic activity. For instance, pinning the initial date of a Martian volcano to the date of a mass extinction would constitute telling evidence, and a sequence of matching dates from Martian stratigraphy would be even more persuasive. The double extinctions of Late Devonian and Permian eons,

---

[36] D.J. McLaren, "Time, life, and boundaries," *Journal of Paleontology* 44 (1970): 801-15, cited in A. Hallam and P.B. Wignall, *Mass Extinctions and Their Aftermath* (New York: Oxford University Press, 1997), 85

[37] Roberto A. Scasso *et al.*, "A tsunami deposit at the Cretaceous/Paleogene boundary in the Neuquén Basin of Argentina," *Cretaceous Research* 26 (2005): 283-297

[38] See, for instance, Eduardo A.M. Koutsoukos, "An extraterrestrial impact in the early Danian: a secondary K/T boundary event?" *Terra Nova* 10, 1998: 68-73

for instance, might be matched with a parallel pattern in Martian volcanoes, and other patterns on Mars may fit the contours and idiosyncrasies of the great mass extinctions on Earth. Meanwhile, Hellas depression at the antipodes of the Tharsis region, while clearly formed by an impact that scattered debris for 4000 km, could conceivably have been deepened, as the most vulnerable part of the antipodes, by the Earth's gravitational pull on the opposite side of Mars. This would account for its exceptional depth (8200 meters).

Third, given the possibility that during some encounters Mars would have come close to the Moon, a search on the Moon also might yield evidence. In particular, the large maria formed by lava flows on the Moon might have been caused in part by early close encounters of the Moon, as well as the Earth, with the Red Planet. The disproportion between their presence on the near side (31.2 % of its surface) and the far side (2.5%) has defied explanation. But a report[39] of domes ranging from less than 1 km to more than 6 km, some with steeply sloping sides, in the Compton-Belkovich thorium anomaly on the far side suggests that the gravitational pull of a passing Mars could have uplifted the domes; and it might have caused the lava flows that formed the few maria as well. In other words, pulled by Earth's gravitational field, Mars tended to pass between Earth and Moon during encounters; but occasionally it presumably passed outside of the Moon. The finding of major spikes in the past 400 million years in the numbers of lunar spherules, some from pyroclastic eruptions, would also be consistent with approaches by Mars.[40] Again, the Bronze Age approaches of Venus to Earth could have affected the surface of the Moon as well.

Fourth, we can hunt for evidence that Earth pulled matter from Mars during close approaches. For instance, the extraterrestrial origin of

---

[39] Bradley L. Jolliff *et al.* "Non-mare silicic volcanism on the lunar farside at Compton-Belkovich," *Nature Geoscience* online, 24 July 2011, www.nature.com/ngeo/journal/vapo/ncurrent/full/ngeo1212.html

[40] Richard A. Muller, "Measurement of the lunar impact record for the past 3.5 b.y. and implications for the Nemesis theory," in: Christian Koeberl and Kenneth G. MacLeod, eds., *Catastrophic Events and Mass Extinctions: Impacts and Beyond* (Boulder CO: Geological Society of America, 2002), 659-65

Buckyballs in one report[41] might have been Mars, and other finds of matter on Earth of Martian origin may be tied to the dates of presumed approaches.

Fifth, we need to study the questions of celestial mechanics that MTME raises.

Why the MTME?

Why should we think that the Martian Theory of Mass Extinctions is the long-sought solution to the mystery of the mass extinctions?

1. Close approaches of Mars would have had the requisite power to set off tremendous seismic and volcanic activity, which entraining the other phenomena associated with extinctions. Rapid inversions would add worldwide, continent-sweeping tsunamis as a kill mechanism.
2. The MTME fits the irregularly occurring but repeated pattern of the mass extinctions.
3. MTME explains why the five great mass extinctions differed from each other: the differences arose from the number of repeated approaches of Mars and from how close Mars came to Earth.
4. The colossal volcanoes and uplifted Tharsis region of Mars are consistent with repeated encounters with Earth, and the time range seems right.
5. A body of evidence and theory about the approaches of Venus and Mars in the Bronze and Iron Ages parallels what is known about the mass extinctions.
6. Approaches by Mars would perfectly fulfill the apparent criterion of a powerful perpetrator who committed the crime, then disappeared without leaving a single footprint—and then returned

---

[41] L. Becker et al., "Impact Event at the Permian-Triassic Boundary: Evidence from Extraterrestrial Noble Gases in Fullerenes," *Science* 291 (2001): 1530-33, cited in Peter Ward and Joe Kirschvink, *A New History of Life* (New York: Bloomsbury Press, 2015), 216-7

to the scene of the crime to commit another and another and another.[42]

---

[42] See also Richard A. Day, "A Roche-Limit Encounter Explains Martian Features," Society for Scientific Exploration paper, 2000, delivered as a presentation at an SSE conference in Toronto. The complete paper has thus far eluded retrieval. Here is the abstract:

Mars has surface features that are not seen on inner planets or moons. These are hemispheric asymmetries, idiosyncratic surface fracturing, localized vulcanism, altitude differences, chains of pits, and the nature of dry river-like channels. Other features include extensive loss of an early atmosphere and liquid water. There is interest in the lower-altitude northern region, with its surface formed after the period of heavy bombardment, as a possible ocean basin. The evidence for this is very sparse: no river deltas, no river networks, little debris at the ends of the catastrophic flow channels. The surface is consistent with the stripping anticipated by a Roche-limit encounter. The low-density Martian moons appear to be unconsolidated material of higher density; they appear to be from low-gravity aggregation of that part of the Martian debris that went into orbit as a short-lived ring. A Roche-limit encounter is invoked as a reasonable hypothesis to explain these features. Earth, Mars' nearest planetary neighbor, may have provided that encounter. The Roche limit is 2.9 Earth radii.

Chapter 4

Theory of the Reversing Earth

There are good reasons to think that Earth has turned over on various occasions. But who can be surprised that this notion—so removed from everyday experience and common sense—seems less than instantaneously persuasive?

The good reasons include telling evidence in narrative testimony and correctly interpreted myths of the ancients, embedded patterns in ancient cultures that give evidence of inversions, and the insights and arguments of two formidable researchers. Now we can 1) add new reasons that strengthen the case; 2) specify the approximate dates of four inversions; 3) comprehend that Earth is actually prone to inversion; and 4) point to where to find more evidence. We can also see that understanding inversions helps us correct errors in interpreting past planetary and Earth science, including the history of climate change.

Ancient Sources and Velikovsky

Herodotus wrote that Egyptian priests had told him that four times since Egypt became a kingdom "the Sun rose contrary to his wont; twice he rose where he now sets, and twice he set where he now rises." The Egyptians had a name for the Sun when it rose in the west, "Re-Horakhty". Horakhty meant "Horus of the Two Horizons". This is commonly interpreted as referring to the rising and setting of the Sun, but in fact it meant that the Sun possessed the capability of rising in both east and west. The concept of the Sun rising in the west occurs in both Christian and Muslim literature. The reversal also appears in Greek literature, most notably in the *Statesman* of Plato.

As we saw in Chapter 1, in *Worlds in Collision* Immanuel Velikovsky interpreted this evidence, and much else, in connection with his theory that Venus had emerged from Jupiter and approached Earth every 52 years during the Bronze Age. On four occasions Venus came close enough to cause super-catastrophes. It was during these close approaches that Earth turned over. Velikovsky ascribed this to electromagnetic forces, and they very possibly played some role; but gravitational interaction seems a more likely main cause.

In addition to ancient testimony, Velikovsky found further evidence of reversals. The Chinese zodiac is retrograde. The name Arab derives from the word for the setting of the Sun, so that that the Arabs, as seen from the Levant, were the people of the setting Sun. Egyptian administrator Senenmut (Senmut) had a section of the ceiling of his tomb painted with a stellar array that was retrograde, matching a world that had inverted. In other words, the evidence goes beyond written narratives and rather easy-to-interpret myths. As pointed out in Chapter 1, the evidence also is too plentiful and telling to be outweighed by exaggerated counterfactual objections, e.g., that such an inversion would have created a colossal flooding of Earth's entire landmass, for which there is no evidence. In fact, there is plenty of evidence (e.g., the skeleton of a whale found far inland near Anyang, China) of lesser but still gigantic tsunamis that were evidently set off by inversions that took place over ten days, thereby mitigating the inertial effect that a more rapid inversion would have had on the oceans.

In effect, therefore, the first two stages of the Reversing Earth theory—the ancient sources and Immanuel Velikovsky—provide good reasons to think that Earth had inverted in a very specific manner. Still, Velikovsky did not offer a clear scientific mechanism for the inversions.

The Theory's Third Stage

In a third stage of development, British researcher Peter Warlow devised an explanation of the mechanism of inversion. Warlow argued that Earth resembled a kind of top termed a tippe top, which turns itself over when sufficient torque is applied to its axis. But when Warlow published his hypothesis in a scientific journal, his methods and conclusions were severely criticized.[43] Faulting Warlow's mathematics, his critic, Victor J. Slabinski, wrote that the required torque to cause an inversion of Earth would have to come from a body at least 417 times the mass of Earth, among other objections. Slabinski's arguments drew a well-argued counterattack from David Salkeld.[44] Still, Slabinski's criticism obliged Warlow to rethink his arguments. Eventually he published a book, *The Reversing Earth*,[45] that provided a more persuasive mechanism.

Figure 4. Tippe Top

Warlow argued that we need to separate the spin of Earth from its body. In a tippe top model, upon the approach of a planet like Venus or Mars, even as the spin continued with only a small diminution, a modest torque would set off a fast precession of the body whereby the body would invert 180 degrees in several stages in as little as a day or two. This inversion would take place along Earth's "secondary equator" between its land and ocean hemispheres, roughly at 60°W and 120°E.

Warlow further contended that there is no such thing as a geomagnetic reversal. Attached to Earth's spin, the geomagnetic field would remain pointed in the same direction, albeit temporarily dipping to an intensity of perhaps 15 percent. He claimed to find evidence for various magnetic reversals (inversions, in his thinking) in the geological record, but over time it has become clear that there is little evidence for geomagnetic reversals during the crucial Bronze Age catastrophes. In fact, we now

---

[43] P. Warlow, "Geomagnetic reversals?" *Journal of Physics A: Mathematical and General* 11 (1978), No. 10: 2107-2130; Victor J. Slabinski, "A dynamical objection to the inversion of the Earth on its spin axis," Ibid., No. 14 (1981): 2503-2507
[44] http://www.sis-group.org.uk/files/docs/1989-objections-overruled.pdf
[45] London: J.M. Dent & Sons, 1982

know that the geomagnetic field is connected to Earth's body, not its spin; the center of the field is located at 25°N, 153°E in the direction of the northwest Pacific, and it has been approximately in this position for hundreds of millions of years.[46] Thus it is somehow connected to the solid body of Earth, and during an inversion it would invert along with the body. Therefore, geomagnetic reversals are not linked to inversions of Earth.

Curiously, the demise of Warlow's magnetic reversal hypothesis (that there were no geomagnetic reversals) actually strengthened his fast precession theory of inversions because it no longer faced the lack of evidence of geomagnetic reversals during the Bronze Age catastrophes (the main exception being several pieces of Etruscan and Greek pottery). Also, we no longer have to posit thousands of inversions caused, presumably, by thousands of approaches of heavenly bodies, to match the thousands of magnetic reversals on the record.

Warlow's book also offered rich evidence and analysis that went beyond Velikovsky, for instance, in specifying exactly how Plato included evidence of inversion drawn from tradition in his *Statesman*, even though he misunderstood it. In addition, Warlow provided a perceptive account of how humans undergoing inversion would think about it.

Stage 4

With the removal of magnetic reversals from the discussion and recognition of Warlow's true contributions, we have entered the fourth stage of the development of the theory of inversions. We now also have a better understanding of why Earth seems so labile, so prone to tipping over: as discussed in Chapter 2, when Terramars passed Jupiter, tidal heating turned it molten, and Jupiter's gravity extracted Mars from the Pacific Basin. Even though Earth's surface was over time restored to a

---

[46] William Lowrie, *A Student's Guide to Geophysical Equations* (Cambridge: Cambridge University Press, 2011), 211-212

nearly spherical contour, the deep scar created an anomaly in Earth reaching down some 2700 km, and thus made Earth unusually unstable.[47]

This helps to explain why just a brief interaction with a passing planet can set off the fast precession/toppling that Warlow describes. What portion of the effect is caused by the tippe top phenomenon and what portion by the scar left by Mars is difficult to determine. At any rate we can see that, far from being a rigid, smooth, round billiard ball, Earth is a lopsided, unstable, wobbly spheroid that can in chaotic fashion topple over in response to a relatively minor torque.

In a more general sense, we can say that the Reversing Earth theory has also gained momentum from new evidence and reinterpretation supporting Velikovsky's Venus theory (Chapter 1), the related Outer Solar System Origin of the Terrestrial Planets theory (OSSO) (Chapter 2), and the more distantly related Martian Theory of Mass Extinctions (Chapter 3). These theories are all mutually supportive, so telling evidence in one supports the others.

It is likely that the closest of these approaches of Mars also caused inversions of Earth, and that these were much faster (presumably because Mars had practically struck Earth) and thus much more devastating than the Bronze Age inversions, each of which seems to have occurred over a period of ten days. Each rapid inversion would have included gigantic tsunamis that profoundly upturned the water column and inundated the land, explaining better than anything else the exceptional devastation of the mass extinctions. As pointed out in Chapter 3, evidence of such tsunamis has been mistakenly attributed to bolide impacts. Repeated very close approaches of Mars could have caused several inversions in a row, while the rapidity and hence the destructiveness of the inversion could have been related to the closeness of approach, which would explain why the largest five mass extinctions differed in extent.

---

[47] This explanation of the geology of the Pacific Basin neatly meshes with the model of Earth's mantle as marked by extensive networks of plumes underlying hotspots in the Pacific and the antipodal African regions in V. Courtillot *et al.*, "Three different types of hotspots in the Earth's mantle," *Earth and Planetary Science Letters*, vol. 166 (2003): 295-308.

Where can we seek new evidence? Because circulation of seas and lakes changed direction relative to the shores during inversions, it might prove possible to find evidence of a switch in direction in ocean sediments and lake varves. Very likely, Bronze Age archaeological sites also contain much more valuable information about inversions, e.g., burial orientations. Another promising area is the orientation of temples and other buildings. For instance (see Chapter 5), the original orientation of the temple of Amun-Re at Karnak aimed at the rising summer solstice Sun during the First Intermediate Period and early Middle Kingdom (around 2050-1950 BC) in an era when the Sun rose in the west. Then, after another inversion, New Kingdom pharaohs built chapels, windows, and even a mini-temple to view the rising winter solstice Sun in the east.

Meanwhile, the dates of Venus' first approach and the first two inversions neatly fit the construction phases and intricate patterns of stones at Stonehenge (see Chapter 9). We now can also see that the appearance of the Earth's shadow starting on the west of the Moon, cited as a particularly dangerous omen by the Babylonians, seems to have originated during an epoch of an inverted Earth.

In China, the myth of Archer Yi who, with his vermilion bow, shot down nine of ten suns that were making Earth too hot had a variant that the suns were sequential.[48] We can see that this referred to ten successive days on which the Sun followed a different course across the sky during an inversion until Earth reached a 180° inversion and settled on the tenth sun. Archer Yi was Comet-Planet Venus. Its curving twin tails made a reddish (from atmospheric dust) bow, with Venus' body blocking sunlight from the central portion of its tail (as Velikovsky had argued regarding the horns of the Near Eastern, Greek, and South Asian bull of heaven). The bow, directed by the solar wind, tracked the Sun as it emerged in a different location each morning. Ancient sources report the ten suns as an ill omen appearing toward the ends of the Xia and Shang dynasties.[49] We can suppose that they appeared, perhaps partly obscured by atmospheric and planetary dust, toward the ends of the neolithic Longshan period around

---

[48] Sarah Allan, *The Shape of the Turtle: Myth, Art, and Cosmos in Early China* (Albany: SUNY, 1991), 26
[49] Ibid., 38

2200 BC and the Western Zhou dynasty somewhat before 771 BC as well.[50] While Shang was characterized in myth as eastern, the Xia dynasty was characterized as western.[51] This would presumably apply to the Western Zhou dynasty as well, i.e., Xia and Western Zhou were times when the Sun and Venus rose in the west.

The east-west pattern of Chinese dynasties supports what the Egyptian priests told Herodotus about the Sun rising twice in the west and setting twice in the east: clearly, they meant that there were four inversions. As the Aztecs put it, we now live in the age of the Fifth Sun.

Thus the various findings and theoretical explanations in Stages 3 and 4 of the Theory of the Reversing Earth make it increasingly difficult to deny that Earth has a built-in capacity for inversion, that it has indeed turned over upon occasion, and that it may turn over again.

---

[50] The first inversion was the 4.2 ka event around 2200 BC. According to dendrochronology, the second seems to have been around 1628 BC; see Mike Baillie, *Exodus to Arthur: Catastrophic Encounters with Comets* (London: B.T. Batsford, 1999), 53-54. This seems consistent with a Chinese report of a ten-sun episode in 1615 BC (the dating of Chinese annals is inexact, as are the Egyptian chronology-based Western dates): Sean Mewhinney, "On 'the Year -687'", *Kronos*, Vol. VI, No. 4 (1981): 4-27. The last two were around 1210 and 820 BC; see David Kaniewski *et al.*, "Environmental Roots of the Late Bronze Age Crisis," *PLoS ONE* 8(8): e71004 (2013). Clearly, the inversions could precede the final collapse of the dynasties by many decades; and in other encounters on a 52-year cycle Venus jerked Earth enough to disrupt the climate and damage the kingdoms, though without inversions and gigantic tsunamis. Studies that parallel Kaniewski *et al.* should be a high priority, with the hypothesis/prediction that climatological shifts similar to those for 1210 and 820 BC will be found around 2200 and 1628 BC. In general, estimates of the dates of the four inversions place us in a much better position to identify and interpret corroborating evidence.

[51] Allan, 64. This appears to go beyond the simple fact that the capital cities were relatively speaking eastern and western.

Chapter 5

Evidence from Egypt

Velikovsky's Venus and Reversing Earth theories drew heavily on Egyptian evidence. New findings strengthen the case and enable us to penetrate several major enigmas of ancient Egypt. Here we will discuss the Great Sphinx, the orientation of the Temple of Amon-Re at Karnak, the famous lioness goddess Sekhmet, and the statues of Ramses II and Nefertari at Abu Simbel.

Why the Sphinx?

Figure 5. The Great Sphinx

Among the deepest mysteries of ancient Egypt is the Great Sphinx of Giza. Researchers have painstakingly investigated its every aspect. Yet key puzzles remain, above all the question of why this colossal structure was built in the first place.

Serious researchers and free-ranging speculators have proposed all kinds of explanations. But every theory put forward falls well short of true persuasiveness or stumbles over inconvenient facts. Here are three anomalies a correct theory should explain.

First, why is the Sphinx so much longer than a real lion or than other sphinxes? Some Egyptologists explain this as necessitated by weakness in the rock structure, but that explanation does not address the possibility that the elongation might convey some meaning. It also doesn't account for the length of the paws that stretch out to the front. In addition, several observers have suggested that something originally was located in between or in front of the paws. Later, various structures were inserted there, so we will probably never know for sure. But such an object might have made the monument even longer.

Second, remnants of red ochre-hued paint have been traced back to painting of the Sphinx long after its original construction as it came to be a major monument to Re Horakhty, the Sun god Horus of the Two Horizons. It seems reasonable to suppose that the Sphinx was painted red initially, and that the later painting simply renewed its known color. But why red? Lions are not red.

Third, why would anyone conceive of this project and wish to build it? Is there something about the date of the original construction of the Sphinx that fits both the elongation and the redness? Was something going on that would motivate a king to order such a gigantic monument to be built?

Dating the Sphinx has long been the subject of controversy. Most Egyptologists cite inscriptions, statuary, and other evidence connecting the pyramid behind the Sphinx and the associated temples with Khafre (Cephren). A generally reliable source dates his reign to 2520-2494 BC.[52] They interpret the prior quarrying of the nearby stone for Khufu's earlier pyramid and the close-by undisturbed causeway to Khafre's pyramid as meaning that the Sphinx was built during his reign. Most think that the Sphinx's face, now minus the nose, is probably his. Various Egyptologists hold that it could have been finished under Khafre's successors, and a few have argued that it might have been initially constructed earlier in the IVth Dynasty.

---

[52] John Baines and Jaromír Málek, *The Cultural Atlas of the World: Ancient Egypt* (Oxford: Stonehenge Press, 1984), 36

The main serious scholarly challenge to the professional consensus was mounted by geologist Robert Schoch, who argued that the monument's exterior shows signs of major water damage from rainfall that must have occurred in previous millennia, given the dry climate of Giza at and since the building of the great pyramids. But critics, including geologists, have noted that the Sphinx's near-burial in moist sand could have done the damage, that dew causes ongoing limestone flaking, that the area was wetter at the time of the construction of the pyramids and only turned drier several centuries later, and that occasional rains still fall.[53] It is hard to find an Egyptologist who accepts Schoch's arguments and chronology.

Since late antiquity casual observers, dedicated amateur researchers, psychics, and others have claimed that hidden chambers beneath the Sphinx contain secret writings. In the current main such theory, the construction goes back to 10500 BC when the original pyramids later attributed to Khufu, Khafre, and Menkaure were supposedly aligned to imitate the three stars of Orion's belt. This theory argues that these pyramids and the original ancestor of the Sphinx were built by a superior civilization (some say Atlantis), and that the present Sphinx represents a remodeling of the original one.[54] Professional Egyptologists unanimously reject this, but it resonates with people of a certain outlook.

Clearly, it would be helpful to arrive at a fully persuasive explanation of the Sphinx. In fact, there is one, but it requires understanding what was going on around the world when the Sphinx was built.

A Key Reinterpretation

Immanuel Velikovsky thought that Venus first approached Earth around 1500 BC, but now we know that it was shortly before 2500 BC— the time that the Sphinx was constructed, according to the evidence assembled by the Egyptologists. The initial interaction between Venus and Earth evidently stirred up a great deal of interplanetary dust from

---

[53] Peter James and Nick Thorpe, *Ancient Mysteries* (New York: Ballantine Books, 1999): 223-226
[54] Paul Jordan, *Riddles of the Sphinx* (New York: NYU Press, 1998), 128 ff

Venus' tail as well as dust in Earth's atmosphere. These made Venus look red, as it appears in iconography. The shock of interaction and the appearance of a giant red comet rising in the east would have inspired awe and put fear into millions of people worldwide, including Khafre.

Thus, according to this explanation, Khafre ordered the construction of a gigantic effigy of Venus facing eastward toward the rising planet-comet in front of his pyramid, using the rock next to Khufu's quarry. Khafre had a big ego; the name of his pyramid was "Khafre is great". So it seems that the face of the Sphinx was Khafre's.

As an effigy, the purpose of the Sphinx appears to have been to signal to Venus above that Khafre and his people were devoted to the planet-comet god, to say "We're on your team! Please spare us." This explains why the Sphinx was so large and why it imitated Comet Venus in length and color. But the imitation went farther. As we have seen, the body of Comet Venus blocked sunlight from the center of its tail, at least immediately behind the planet-comet, so that what appeared were two shining trails on the sides. The peoples of the Near East saw them as horns and called Venus the bull of heaven. In Egypt Venus became the preexisting cow goddess Hathor (later it was also assigned to Isis, and over time Hathor merged into Isis), as in this depiction of Khafre's successor Menkaure, between his wife and Hathor. (This depiction has added importance as part of the evidence that Venus had appeared as a comet by the date of Menkaure, very approximately 2500 BC.)

Figure 6. Menkaure with Wife and Hathor

In the headdresses of Egyptian queens, two thick bars imitated the double tail of Venus, as in this image of Nefertari (ca 1250 BC) being led by Isis. The horns on the head of Isis and the reddish oval nested in them denote Venus as well, with the redness coming from the high iron content of the comet and atmospheric dust. Note that the red ball in Nefertari's headdress is more spherical, while that in Isis' headdress is oval.

As we have seen, in ancient times Venus was ovoid, as depicted in iconography and in the layouts of astronomical sites, because it had turned molten while passing Jupiter and was almost pulled in two by Jupiter's gravity. However, because Venus was never far from the Sun, because over the centuries it gradually lost its tail in encounters with Earth and Mars and became more spherical, and because over time cultural amnesia caused memory loss, Venus could easily be overshadowed by the Sun. So early depictions of Venus as a red oval were gradually replaced in iconography by red spheroids interpreted as suns.

Figure 7. Nefertari and Isis

Thus we can construe the long front paws of the Sphinx as the double tail of Venus, as in the queens' headdresses. This suggests that there was a red oval (Venus) in front of the paws. In between the paws is an empty, darker area, as with the darkened central portion of Venus' tail immediately behind the body of the planet. The remaining long body of the Sphinx represented the merging of the twin tails behind the dark area. This hardly constitutes proof that there was an original ovoid depiction of Venus in front of the Sphinx's paws. But, even though assuming that it was indeed there is not required to accept the Venus effigy interpretation of the Sphinx, the notion certainly seems suggestive.

As far as dating the Sphinx is concerned, the Venus effigy interpretation supports Egyptologists' ascription of the Sphinx to Khafre, or just before 2500 BC. The construction of the main megalithic stage of Stonehenge in the years around 2500 BC further buttresses this finding because we now know that Stonehenge included an effigy of Venus and an oval (Chapter 9). In addition, various observers have noted that in Khufu's Great Pyramid, generally of excellent quality stonework, some of the presumably late construction seems downright shoddy, and even some well-built parts were never brought to a logical conclusion. Meanwhile, Khafre's pyramid also uses high-quality stones and construction for the initial several courses, but from there on the construction materials are poor.[55] It seems reasonable to think that the late construction stage of Khufu's pyramid coincided with the early stage of Khafre's, and that a catastrophic approach of Venus around 2525-2520 BC disrupted the construction of both pyramids and perhaps killed or incapacitated the master architect(s) and leading craftsmen, leading to a sharp decline in quality.

Catastrophes caused by approaches of Venus every 52 years may have deposited volcanic ash that, mixed with dew, caused leaching of the surface of the Sphinx, as Schoch and others argue.

Meanwhile, the Sphinx Temple in front of the Sphinx uniquely among Egyptian monuments contains two sanctuaries.[56] We can surmise that they were for the Morning Star and Evening Star, the two ways that Venus presented itself and was worshipped.

Re Horakhty

If Venus made such an impression when it first approached Earth, why did the Sphinx lose its association with Venus over time? One reason has already been suggested—that the Sun appropriated functions and symbols of Venus. But something else also occurred.

From the time of the catastrophic first inversion of Earth around 2200 BC, the Sun and Venus began to rise in the west. They continued to do so throughout the First Intermediate Period and the Middle Kingdom until

---

[55] John Anthony West in Graham Hancock, *Fingerprints of the Gods* (New York: Three Rivers, 1995), 424
[56] Richard H. Wilkinson, *The Complete Temples of Ancient Egypt* (New York: Thames & Hudson, 2000), 18

the second inversion around 1628 BC, when they switched back to rising in the east. During this long western-rising period, the Sphinx became the center of the new cult of Re Horakhty, Horus of the Two Horizons. As previously noted, this name is commonly taken to refer to the Sun rising in the east and setting in the west, but in the context of inversions it refers rather to the Sun that was capable of rising in either the east or the west. It thus became the term for the Sun when it rose in the west. No longer pointing in the right direction to greet the rising Venus, the Sphinx lost its connection to Venus; the loss of tradition in the turmoil of the First Intermediate Period also played a role. Instead, the Sphinx came to be seen as the embodiment of the western-rising Sun, Re Horakhty, facing east as he moved eastward.

Meanwhile, the famous temple of Karnak also bears silent witness.

Karnak, Temple of the Western-Rising Sun

Before beginning to examine the remarkable orientation of the Great Temple of Amon-Re at Karnak in Upper Egypt, we need to see how the approximate dates for the four inversions of Earth—2200, 1628, 1210, and 820 BC—matched the chronology of the dynasties of Egypt.

- During the Old Kingdom (2686-2160 BC), which came to an end soon after the ca 2200 BC inversion, the Sun rose in the east.
- After the first inversion of circa 2200 BC, during the First Intermediate Period (2160-2055 BC) and Middle Kingdom (2055 BC-1650 BC), the Sun rose in the west.
- After the second inversion around 1628 BC (or possibly 1680 BC—this inversion is the least well dated) came the Second Intermediate Period (1650-1550 BC) and early New Kingdom (1550-1210 BC) when the Sun rose in the east. (Both Egyptian chronology and the estimated dates of inversions are approximate, accounting for minor discrepancies such as 1650 versus 1628 BC. Also, some dynasties were able to hang on for decades amid chaos before coming to an end.)

- After the third inversion around 1210 BC came the Third Intermediate Period (1069-664 BC). The Sun rose in the west until 820 BC.
- From 820 BC on, the Sun rose in the east.

Karnak, just north of Thebes, was the greatest temple complex in ancient Egypt, the center of Egyptian religion during the second millennium BC. The exact date of its original construction is unknown, but was in the period of 2050-1950 BC, at the end of the First Intermediate Period. The Great Temple of Amon-Re is built along an axis that runs from WNW to ESE, perpendicular to an old channel of the Nile and across from the Theban Hills on the West Bank.

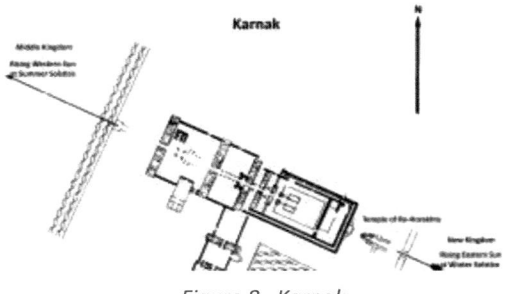

Figure 8. Karnak

In his *The Dawn of Astronomy*,[57] astronomer Norman Lockyer argued that the Great Temple was oriented toward the setting Sun at summer solstice so that the last rays would pass down the axis and illuminate the statue of the god in the sanctuary. However, the rays of the setting Sun were blocked from penetrating the temple along its axis by the Theban Hills on the west bank of the Nile.[58] Later scientists, most notably Gerald Hawkins, identified at least four ways in which the temple appeared to be oriented in the opposite direction, toward the rising Sun at winter solstice.[59] Queen Hatshepsut had a temple built to Amon-Re-who-hears-

---

[57] (London: Cassell, 1894), 117
[58] Ibid., 118
[59] Juan Belmonte, "Karnak", in C.L.N. Ruggles, *Handbook of Archaeoastronomy and Ethnoastronomy*, 3 volumes (New York: Springer, 2015), Vol. 3: 1536. Hawkins wrote: "It is like a Gothic cathedral entered by passing through the great west door, and with the chancel directed toward the east." Gerald Hawkins, *Beyond Stonehenge* (New York: Harper & Row, 1973), 207. He was right, and how we interpret Karnak has implications for the orientations of many European churches and other buildings around the world.

the-prayers facing ESE; it backed onto the original sanctuary oriented toward the WNW. After her death, Tuthmosis III built a Festival Hall facing ESE that blocked her temple. The Hall contained a chapel up a flight of stairs that opened to the east; Hawkins dubbed this the High Room of the Sun. Ramses II added a separate Temple of Re Horakhty along the line of the axis and oriented ESE (Lockyer had already identified this).[60]

Thus some researchers have held that the real orientation of the overall temple was to the east. However, that leaves the evident original orientation toward the west unexplained.

Theory to the Rescue

According to the Theory of the Reversing Earth, the explanation is simple: the temple was originally constructed at the outset of the Middle Kingdom, a time of the western-rising Sun. It was oriented toward the WNW so that the first rays of the rising Sun at the summer solstice (departing from the traditional rising Sun at the winter solstice) penetrated down the axis to illuminate the statue of the god. However, that leaves a different question unanswered: How would they penetrate if they were blocked by the Theban Hills? The answer seems to be that the western-rising Sun at the outset of the Middle Kingdom had a slightly different trajectory than the setting eastern-rising Sun that Lockyer proposed, so that by the time its rays surmounted the Theban Hills it was farther along its trajectory from a notional level horizon. It may be possible to test this scenario with a laser, though the Ptolemaic Great Pylons at the western end are skewed northward, thus blocking the light.[61]

At any rate, it seems clear that the return to an eastern-rising Sun after the ca 1628 BC (or 1680 BC) inversion led to the four attempts during the New Kingdom to provide a structure oriented toward the ESE. These efforts ceased at the time of the ca 1210 BC inversion and return to a western-rising Sun until an inscription dated ca 840 BC, which said: "One

---

[60] Ramses II was perhaps being careful to honor Re's identity as the western-rising Sun even as he oriented his temple toward the east.
[61] Lockyer, 118

climbs the *Aha*, the lonesome place of the majestic soul, the high room [the High Room of the Sun] of the intelligence which moves across the sky; one now opens the door of the horizon building of the primordial god of the two countries in order to see the mystery of Horus shining."[62] This can perhaps best be interpreted as more properly dated a decade or two later and as having the purpose of expressing bewonderment at and reverence for the new eastern-rising Sun after the inversion of ca 820 BC (which itself might have occurred a decade or two earlier).

In northern Egypt, at least two temples built after the ca 1210 BC inversion appear to be oriented like Karnak toward the western-rising Sun. The Temple of Amon-Re at Tanis is oriented toward the WSW, the winter solstice at sunrise of the western-rising Sun (one could, of course, argue that it was the setting of the eastern-rising Sun; but that event has dramatically less significance as the dying of the old year than the sunrise betokening a new year would have; besides, it would be impossible because the Sun was rising in the west).

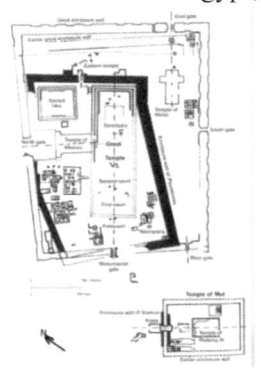

Figure 9. Temple of Amon-Re at Tanis

The western extension of the Temple of Hathor at Serabit el Khadim, apparently built around 1140 BC, deviates from the original orientation of centuries earlier to point at what appears to be the same WSW direction as the temple at Tanis, which would be the winter solstice at sunrise of the western-rising Sun.

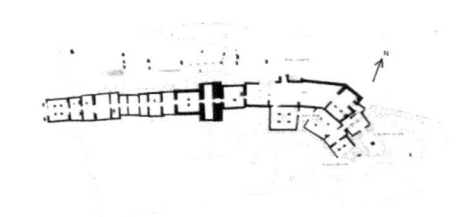

Figure 10. Temple of Hathor at Serabit el Khadim

This account of the orientation of the Great Temple at Karnak has important implications. First, we can see that the theory of inversions enables us much better to understand the rhythm of ancient Egyptian history. In particular, the catastrophes of the three Intermediate Periods gain a powerful triggering cause that fully justifies the lamentation

---

[62] Hawkins, 208

literature and other reports of devastation and chaos. It explains why these episodes so closely resembled each other that scholars have doubted the historicity of the lamentation literature, while investigators like Velikovsky were misled in regard to chronology. Second, Egyptian civilization attained many of its greatest achievements in the teeth of terrible catastrophes. Third, we can better interpret the evolution of Egyptian religion and myth. For example, while the chain of causality leading to Pharaoh Akhenaten's 14th-century BC foundation of a solar-orb monotheistic cult remains obscure, the two previous switches of the Sun between eastern-rising and western-rising must have set people thinking about the Sun itself, and this could have led to Akhenaten's new solar-orb theology. Fourth, understanding Karnak can help us interpret many other ancient orientations around the world, including buildings and open air sites.

Sekhmet, Venus Goddess of Egypt

Like the Great Sphinx and Karnak, Sekhmet ("The Mighty One") can now be properly interpreted. This lion-headed goddess was dreaded for her bloody rampages. Yet she became the protector of kings and a favorite personal goddess of millions of Egyptians.

Why did Egyptians honor a goddess who required such assiduous and even obsessive propitiation? Why did other Egyptian goddesses play roles similar to Sekhmet's? What explains Sekhmet's dual nature as destroyer and protector? Why was she called the Eye of Ra? Why was she originally depicted with an oval disk on her head?

Figure 11. Sekhmet

While Sekhmet frequently received top billing, at times she had to share the stage with other goddesses. These are best understood as thematic or regional variant representations of Comet-Planet Venus. Hathor, the cow goddess of the Old Kingdom, was co-opted into the role of Venus shortly before 2500 BC because her horns matched the twin tails of Venus. At times Hathor was spoken of as an avenging destroyer, or the goddess was be termed Hathor-Sekhmet.

Bastet, the cat goddess of Lower Egypt, was occasionally given a lion head and spoken of as a devastator. But more often she was seen as the benign counterpart of the dangerous Sekhmet: "Sekhmet of yesterday, Bastet of today", as a hymn from Ptolemaic Edfu put it.[63] This suggests a distinction between the Evening Star, which on occasion approached and wreaked havoc, and the Morning Star, which many ancient peoples viewed as harmless. Various temples contained two goddesses representing the aggressive and the peaceful forms of the Eye of Ra (Venus), as with Satet and Anuket at Aswan or Ayet and Nehemtawy at Herakleopolis.[64] Sekhmet, for her part, seems to have been primarily the Evening Star, but sometimes she stood for Venus in general and thus had two sides to her nature. Her cult seems to have begun at Memphis during the Fifth Dynasty, i.e., not long after the first approach of Venus around 2525 BC. Sekhmet's husband was Ptah.

As consort of Amun, Mut seems to have been a regional Venus goddess. She came to be seen as the mother of Sekhmet and gradually assimilated with Sekhmet, hence the roughly 700 statues of Sekhmet at the Precinct of Mut at Karnak (placed next to the Sun god's temple just as Venus accompanied the Sun). The idea seems to have been to provide two statues for each day of the year, to worship the Morning Star and the Evening Star.

Tefnut and other regional lion-headed goddesses replicated Sekhmet's characteristics and were often linked to her. Isis became increasingly important over time and finally assimilated Hathor as a nurturing mother

---

[63] Philippe Germond, *Sekhmet et la protection du monde* (Basel: Éditions de Belles Lettres, 1981), 113
[64] Geraldine Pinch, *Egyptian Mythology* (New York: Oxford University Press, 2002), 130

Venus goddess. Isis and Sekhmet were both said to be the mother of Horus.[65]

Protector of Ra, Kings, and Cosmic Order

Repeated catastrophic approaches of Venus led the Egyptians to endeavor to channel Sekhmet's capacity for destruction into the role of a powerful protector. She was placed at the prow of the solar bark as it entered the underworld every night so that she could protect the Sun against his enemy Apophis. The ceremonies of the New Year contained sedulous efforts to appease Sekhmet for fear that she might unleash the evil power of the five epagomenal days added to 360 at the end of the old year.

Just as the king derived his power from Ra and emulated him, so Sekhmet protected the king. Sekhmet was depicted suckling the king, and kings began to proclaim themselves sons of Sekhmet. Through her protection of the king, who was responsible for maintaining the cosmic order, Sekhmet was seen as the protector of the cosmic order itself. Thus at every occasion it was essential to placate Sekhmet. Otherwise, she might run amok, her hot breath spreading fire and pestilence. Meanwhile, the king relied on Sekhmet to smite his enemies, foreign and domestic.

Two myths sprang up around Sekhmet.

In The Distant Goddess myth, Sekhmet wandered off to the Nubian desert, so Ra sent messengers to persuade her to return. When she did, she flew into a rage because Ra had found a replacement for her as his Eye. To placate her, Ra placed Sekhmet/the Eye on his forehead in the form of a serpent or cobra, the uraeus, which was to govern the entire world.[66] The serpent or cobra, of course, was a fitting incarnation of a comet-planet that preceded the Sun, while the Eye of Ra referred to the oval shape of the Sun's companion Venus.

---

[65] Sigrid-Eike Hoenes, *Untersuchungen zu Wesen und Kult der Göttin Sachmet* (Bonn: R. Habelt Verlag, 1978), 191
[66] Germond, 125

The distancing of Sekhmet could allude to the disappearances of Venus at Superior Conjunction and Inferior Conjunction, or it might have referred to its approaches to Earth.

In a second myth, The Destruction of Men, Ra grew old, and men began to plot against him, withdrawing to the desert. Ra sent his Eye in the form of Hathor who, as a furious lioness, proceeded to slaughter them. Not wanting to exterminate humans, Ra had a beer made that had the color of blood, and he made it inundate the place of massacre. Hathor (Sekhmet) lapped it up and became drunk, so she stopped killing.

This myth alludes to times when the Sun was seen as growing old (as in Aztec myth) and Venus approached especially close to Earth, leading four times to a catastrophic inversion of Earth and the replacement of the old Sun with a new one.

Iconography

Sekhmet was traditionally depicted with a disk on her head. This began as a distinctly oval disk, but over time, as Venus itself became more spheroid, the disk became circular as well and came to be termed a solar disk.

In her typical frontal view, Sekhmet wore a double wig that reached down to her breasts, representing the twin tails of Comet Venus. Sekhmet's dress was red, and she was called "mistress of the red linen" and the "Scarlet Lady". Red was a common color for Comet Venus worldwide because the atmospheric and interplanetary dust Venus stirred up gave it a reddish hue. As we have seen, the Great Sphinx, which took the form of a lion and thus in some manner related to Sekhmet, was painted red.

Sometimes Sekhmet's outfit has a rosette over each breast,[67] presumably symbolizing the Morning Star and the Evening Star.

Over time Sekhmet became associated with Osiris and the realm of the dead, protecting Osiris in his struggles with Seth. This might be a

---

[67] Richard H. Wilkinson, *The Complete Gods and Goddesses of Ancient Egypt* (London: Thames & Hudson, 2003), 182. Mentions rosettes but not Venus.

reference to Venus lingering in the darkness of the night after sun set, though this requires further investigation.

Sekhmet played a major role in medicine, where she was seen as spreading pestilence; epidemics evidently occurred during catastrophic encounters with Venus. Yet she was nonetheless also invoked as a protector from sickness or protector of the sick. Already during the Old Kingdom, some doctors who used magic to ward off diseases doubled as priests of Sekhmet. Thus Sekhmet became a favorite goddess to petition for recovery from disease. In turn, this role extended into widely popular devotion to Sekhmet among millions of Egyptians, Nubians, and others. Thousands of Sekhmet statuettes, scarabs, amulets, and other good luck charms have come down to us. People exchanged amulets at New Year celebrations and implored Sekhmet to protect health, family, crops, and so on. This practice continued alongside the temple cult of Sekhmet into Roman times, long after Venus had lost its tail in encounters with Earth and Mars, and had circularized its orbit so that it no longer approached Earth.

In recent times, Sekhmet has become a cult figure of New Age religion. But neither her present-day devotees nor Egyptologists seem aware that Sekhmet was in fact Comet-Planet Venus. Sekhmet's is not a story of some fanciful, inconsequential cult figure, but rather a lesson in how a great ancient civilization grappled with an all-too-real and terrifying threat to its existence. The Bronze Age catastrophes that caused the famines and plagues of Egypt, dried up the Nile, toppled dynasties, and spawned a touching lamentation literature were not mere figments of Egyptians' imaginations.

Interpreting Abu Simbel

Before we depart from Egypt, we need to take a look at one more piece of evidence, this time from Abu Simbel.

In this photograph of Pharaoh Ramses II and his consort Nefertari can be seen the comet Venus and its two-pronged tail in Nefertari's headdress. The headdress of Ramses II contains the smaller Mars with its two imperfectly round moons and its own tail, presumably of dust stirred up by an encounter with Venus or borrowed from Venus' tail. How could ancient Egyptians have seen the moons of Mars with the naked eye? How could these headdresses be explained other than as depictions of Venus and Mars during approaches to the Earth?

Figure 12. Ramses II and Nefertari at Abu Simbel

Chapter 6

Venus, the Ancient Near East, and Islam

With new-found confidence that the Ancients and Velikovsky were right about Venus, we can ask: how can we use this knowledge to understand the culture of the Ancient Near East and the background of Islam?

Ishtar, Astarte, Ashur

To start with, we can see a simple explanation of the names Ishtar and Astarte, the great Venus goddesses of the ancient Semites who suddenly appeared around 2500 B.C. (the Sumerian goddess Inanna was coopted for Venus, as was Hathor in Egypt). It seems likely that Semitic speakers picked up the word "star" for the wondrous new comet from their Indo-European neighbors (Farsi, *setareh*; Kurdish, *st'r*; Hittite, *shittar*), transposed letters in a characteristic manner, and ended up with Ishtar, Astarte, Asherah, in Yemen 'Attar/'Astar, a male god, and Dushara of the Nabataeans.[68] (A parallel derivation is the Arabic *Mushtaree* for Jupiter.)

---

[68] The name Ishtar has never been convincingly explained within Semitic linguistics. G. Johannes Botterweck, Helmer Ringgren, and Heinz-Josef Fabry, eds., *Theological Dictionary of the Old Testament* (Grand Rapids, Michigan: William B. Eerdmans Publishing Company, 1987-8), Vol. XI, 423-34

Next, it seems clear that the Egyptian goddess Isis (originally Isi, with the s pronounced as a z) had the same basic name as the Arabic *Al-'Uzza*, the Sublime One, the name of Venus/Ishtar. Thus the long history and wide spread of the cult of Isis in the Roman world forms part of the history of the cult of Venus.

In addition, the supreme deity of the Assyrians, Ashur (for which the Assyrian capital Ashur was named) was at times depicted with two horns (the Bull of Heaven), in other words, as the male version of Venus. Ashur

Figure 13. The Winged Disk

seems to be an Akkadian (Semitic) corruption of Indo-European "star", leaving out the t; a parallel is the Canaanite Asherah for Astarte. Ashur was sometimes depicted as in a disk with two wings (the bifurcated tail of Venus), but usually the disk was left empty, giving rise to the well-known winged disk symbol, which was used extensively by the ancient Egyptians and later by Rosicrucians and others. In addition, we can see that the name Assyria actually meant the Land of Venus, as does modern-day Syria.

Meanwhile, the Sumerian name for Venus, Nibiru, has come to be associated with the suppositious mysterious planet that various seers predicted would collide with the Earth on December 21, 2012 at the end of a cycle of the Mayan Venus calendar. But both the fears of ignorant people and the debunking explanations given by various scientists, who were unaware of the new findings on the Venus theory, were off target. There was indeed a planet named Nibiru in ancient times. It was and is Venus. And, unlike during the Bronze Age catastrophes, it does not now represent any threat to the Earth.

Evidence from Mesopotamia includes several oval temples, evidently designed to catch the attention of Venus as it passed overhead. It also includes the headdress of Shamash in the stele of Hammurabi, which shows a coiled serpent—Comet Venus. This headdress also appears in a depiction of the new Sun (Shamash), which arose in the west, stabbing to death the old Sun. This links an iconographic form of an unknown Mesopotamian myth to many instances worldwide of aging or dying suns—these suns refer to inversions of Earth.

Figure 14. Stele of Hammurabi (top)

Figure 15. Shamash Stabs the Old Sun

Otherwise hard-to-explain phenomena in the history of the Ancient Near East, such as the collapses of the Old, Middle, and New Kingdoms of Egypt associated with the failure of the Nile flood, can be neatly explained as the consequences of particularly close passages of Venus. Earth's shadow, for instance, appeared first on the west of the Moon during eclipses in certain dire Babylonian omens. Yet, even though the Babylonians reported many details of celestial phenomena, the astrologers of Babylon are said not to have relied on actual observations.

According to a leading expert, "The existence of Babylonian omens for eclipses beginning and clearing in all four directions, or areas of the moon, despite the fact that a lunar eclipse will never begin on the western edge of the moon, indicates a lack of concern with observational veracity in favor of schematic order."[69]

But during the two periods when the Earth was "upside down" after inversions, in a lunar eclipse Earth's shadow would have impinged on the Moon starting from the west. We can readily understand that the Babylonian astrologers would have considered this a remarkable, threatening omen in their times, as well as when it was read in the

---

[69] Francesca Rochberg-Halton, *Aspects of Babylonian celestial divination: the lunar eclipse tablets of Enuma Anu Enlil. Archiv für Orientforschung.* Beiheft 22. (Horn, Austria: 1988), 52

following centuries. And their accounts of it would have been very factual—not at all "schematic" or "counterfactual". So scholars must revise their interpretation of the relationship between Babylonian astrology and astronomical observations.

Venus and Islam

What effect did the Venus cult have on early Islam?

First, although much has been made of the sexual nature of Ishtar, in fact she was originally a fearsome goddess of war. The chief goddess of the ancient Semites, Ishtar came to be associated with fertility and thereby acquired sexual attributes. In other words, Ishtar was above all a planetary goddess, a giant comet initially traversing the heavens in an awesome manner. We may surmise that, as Venus slowly lost its tail and became more and more simply a bright planet, and as it circularized its orbit and ceased interacting with the Earth, it ceased to inspire fear. Eventually, led by Mohammed, himself originally an Ishtar-worshipper, the Arabs proved willing to abandon their worship of Venus.

The leading center of the Arabs' Venus cult was the black *Kaaba* stone at Mecca, presumably a meteorite that had fallen from the tail of Venus. Mohammed is said to have ruled that the rituals around the *Kaaba* were a pious practice and could continue as part of the *Haj*.

A well-known symbol of Venus also found its way into Islam: the horns of the Bull of Heaven were placed atop the mosques of the new religion (as in this image of al-Bahr Mosque, Jaffa), though soon the explanation that they represented the crescent of the Moon led many new mosques farther away from Mecca to adopt a configuration of a tilted crescent. (As a parallel, as the eve of Sabbath comes, and with it the appearance of Venus, Jews sing greetings to the Sabbath Queen.)

Figure 16. al-Bahr Mosque, Jaffa

Lastly, a key component of the approaches of Venus—that the Earth turned over four times—evidently entered into Arab folklore only to reemerge as the Islamic teaching that on the Judgment Day the Sun would rise in the west. Then the time of repentance is past. The sentence in Sura

55 of the Koran "Lord of the two Easts, and Lord of the two Wests!" fits the same pattern.

In other words, a correct understanding of the approaches of Venus in the Bronze Age can help us better to understand both the Ancient Near East and the origins of Islam.[70]

Meanwhile, in the mountains to the north of the Fertile Crescent is another remarkable piece of the puzzle.

Karahunj, Armenia a Raptor Bird

On the fringe of the Ancient Near East, Karahunj (Zorats Karer) in southern Armenia is an ancient site that contains more than 230 large stones, some 37 still standing, arranged in a fashion that has suggested to some observers that it was an archaeoastronomy site. But defining how it was used has remained elusive. Complicating the situation, Karahunj is located near a complex of ancient graves; we do not know who built it; it is difficult to ascertain exactly when the stones were set up; and some 85 have holes drilled through them. Some researchers have suggested the holes might be used for sighting celestial objects, but other researchers think this unlikely because they would have been too imprecise.[71]

Figure 17. Karahunj

---

[70] I am indebted to my student Mariam Al-Wazir for the references to the horns of Ashur meaning that he was Venus and to *Mushtaree* (Jupiter) as a Semitic borrowing from the Indo-European "star".

[71] A. César González-García, "Carahunge—A Critical Assessment," In: Ruggles, 1453-1460

The repeated devastating approaches of Venus during the Bronze Age led peoples worldwide to propitiate the fearsome god/goddess by building effigies of Venus that the passing comet could view from above. These Venus sites were also used for tracking the comet and for conducting rituals (at times, human sacrifices) to appease the comet-god. These sites had a number of telltale characteristics that differentiate them from normal solar observatories, though observation of the Sun might also have taken place at such Venus sites.

Karahunj has three such characteristics. First, the stone ring at its center forms an oval. It is sometimes reported as a circle, and on the map appears the tracing of a circle. But we can see that the stones form an oval. When Venus was pulled by Jupiter's gravity into the inner solar system around 2525 BC, tidal heating turned it into a molten, ovoid comet; and it was depicted as an ovoid in many ancient sites.

Second, Venus' large body blacked out the central part of its tail. As we

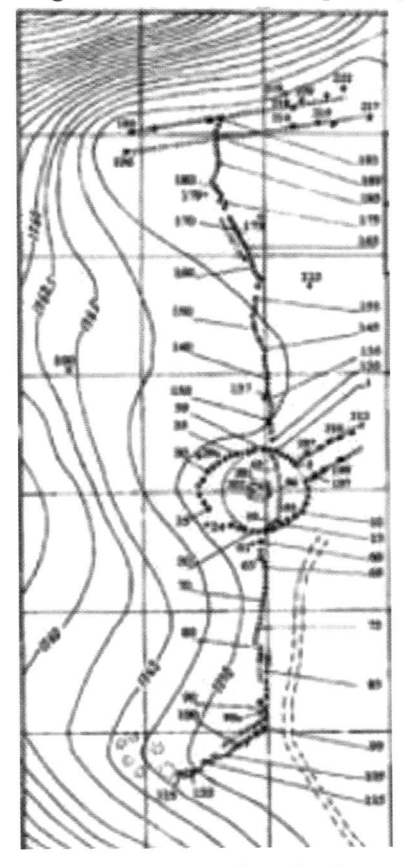

Figure 18. Map of Karahunj

have seen, people in the Near East thought the tail's bright sides were horns, so they called Venus the Bull of Heaven. Similarly, various peoples termed Venus a bird, with bright wings instead of horns. In China, one of its many names was the Vermilion Bird. At Karahunj the stones form a reasonable facsimile of a large raptor bird with long wings, facing east. The right wing bends back at the end; the left one seems at its end to bend forward, or at least to be somehow complex. One interpretation of Karahunj as a bird effigy is that the long straightness of its wings was not based on its actual appearance; the two visible sides of Venus' tail were probably more swept-back than Karahunj shows. Conversely, the builders may have sought to replicate, at the end of the left wing, the complicated configuration of what they saw in the sky at one time; the tail of Venus could have twisted in response to the solar wind.

Third, an alley of stones extends from the oval in a northeast direction. This has been interpreted as aimed at the winter solstice, the major lunistice, or the rising point of Venus. On the map it is evident that in the opposite direction the stone oval is also interrupted, and a single stone stands outside in the center of the direction opposite to the alley. Whether the alley would be used for other purposes, this interpretation would have it primarily intended to track Venus at the horizon.

However, here a tricky question of dating arises. As we have seen in Chapter 4, from 2200 to 1628 BC, Venus would have risen with the Sun in the west. Then, from 1628 to 1210 BC, in the east again. Then from 1210 to 820 BC, in the west again. And finally, after 820 BC, in the east. Can we ascertain the approximate date of Karahunj from how the configuration of stones matched the direction of a rising or setting Venus?

A second tricky question arises from the consideration that Venus appeared as both Morning Star/Comet and Evening Star/Comet. While tracking the rise of Venus in the morning, especially its heliacal rise, was definitely of interest to the ancients, they seem to have considered the Evening Star/Comet as the more dangerous of the two and thus more worth tracking. Also, its last setting along the horizon before it disappeared was farther from the Sun than the rising of the Morning Star/Comet. How do we sort out alignments for the Morning Star from those for the Evening Star as well as distinguishing between rising and setting?

Parallel instances can help us think about the alignments at Karahunj. Taosi site in China was evidently also primarily a Venus observatory; the alignments of its viewing slots make no sense for observing the Sun. When Taosi was operating in the period around 2100 to 1900 BC, Venus was rising in the west. Yet the site is oriented toward the east. This suggests that the Chinese astronomers were tracking the setting points of the Evening Star/Comet (Chapter 8). Another parallel is with Stonehenge, also a Venus site (Chapter 9). A third may be with the alignments at the Minoan palace at Knossos and at several Cretan mountaintop sanctuaries.[72] While these may have been used originally to spot the rising Sun at autumn equinox in the period before 2200 BC, they could have served after the inversion to track not only the setting of the western-rising Sun but also, and with keen interest, the setting of the Evening Star.

Thus Karahunj can perhaps best be interpreted as primarily a Venus observatory site, like Taosi, that was built following the inversion of 2200 BC; and the alley was oriented toward east northeast, the farthest setting point of the Evening Star/Comet. However, the alley may have been wide enough to permit observation of the setting summer solstice Sun as well during eras of a western-rising Sun. While Comet Venus was awe-inspiring, so was a Sun that rose in the west and set in the east.

And the holes in the stones? When the wind blows, they give off a singing sound. As if from a giant bird?

---

[72] G. Henriksson and M. Blomberg, "The Evidence from Knossos on the Minoan Calendar," *Mediterranean Archaeology and Archaeometry*, Vol. 11, No. 1 (2011): 59-68

Chapter 7

Why Topless? Why the Snakes?

Figure 19. Minoan Snake Goddess

The famous Snake Goddess of ancient Crete has long attracted students of history and art. Elegant, *risquée*, enigmatic, she embodies the mystery and allure of Minoan civilization.

Her textbook designation Snake Goddess tells us nothing we couldn't have guessed for ourselves. But perhaps we can get to know her better. She could lead us to evidence and theory that illuminate important patterns in ancient civilization. In effect, calling her merely "Snake Goddess" might represent a Type 2 error, a failure to spot a significant pattern in the information available.

A starting point: we can ask whether there is another image that resembles hers. In fact, at least one depiction of the leading Canaanite goddess Astarte/Asherah shares striking features with the Snake Goddess. Both are topless, and both are holding snakes in their hands. At first glance, Astarte's seem to be plants. But their snake eyes give them away. Then why does Astarte seem to be feeding them to the horses? And why are they cut off beneath her hands?

Figure 20. Astarte with Horses

A second depiction of Astarte shows her actually feeding plants to goats.[73] These plants no longer have snake eyes. The original story of a goddess with snakes in her hands could have made little sense to the artist of the first Astarte, who retained the snakes' eyes but otherwise cut off their tails and introduced the horses in a feeding mode, one that was carried further in the second picture of Astarte, where the horses give way to goats and the half-snakes give way to 100% plants. In turn, this suggests that a conceivable original picture, of which we have no Canaanite instantiation, contains just Astarte holding full-length snakes, exactly as with the Cretan Snake Goddess.

Clearly, the artist who designed the Cretan figurine wanted to depict a goddess holding snakes, and that suggests that this depiction had meaning for him or her, or at least that it faithfully copied an image that had meaning for its creator. So, too, would a putative parallel original depiction of Astarte holding full-length snakes have held meaning for its Canaanite artist. What could that meaning have been?

Astarte was the goddess of the planet Venus—Ishtar in Mesopotamia and elsewhere, al-'Uzza (the Sublime One) among the Arabs, by far the most important female deity of the Ancient Near East. Ishtar/Astarte was the female version of the planet Venus, while the male version of Venus was the Bull of Heaven, of the Gilgamesh epic and other sources.

---

[73] See the cover of Joan Aruz, Kim Benzel, Jean M. Evans, eds. *Beyond Babylon: Art, Trade, and Diplomacy in the Second Millennium B.C.* (New York: Metropolitan Museum of Art, 2008)

Velikovsky noted that "The Egyptian Venus-Isis, the Babylonian Venus-Ishtar, the Greek Venus-Athene were goddesses pictured with serpents, and sometimes represented as dragons."[74] So it seems reasonable to think that the snakes in the hands of the Canaanite Astarte were the female parallel to the horns of the male Bull of Heaven. To the imaginative ancient observer, the divided tail of the comet/planet Venus resembled snakes held in the hands of the goddess. If this is correct, then it follows that the Cretan Snake Goddess was in all likelihood also Astarte, the goddess of the comet/planet Venus.

Why Topless?

An explanation of why the Cretan Snake Goddess is topless can be derived from a similar pattern of change from an original. While she preserves the naked breasts of her Canaanite counterpart, the Cretan lady wears a much more concealing and stylish dress. Even her upper arms are covered. So it could be that the artist strove to preserve the identity of Astarte by retaining the naked breasts but otherwise sought to create a more regal and attractive image of the goddess.

Some backing for this point might be extracted from the Egyptian depiction we encountered in Chapter 5 of Isis leading Nefertari, consort of Pharaoh Ramses II. While both figures are tastefully dressed, Isis seems at least ambiguously topless, or at least her outfit is pretty low-cut. This might be an attempt by the artist to remain true to a characteristic feature of Isis/Astarte while taking care not to offend Nefertari by anything as vulgar as a blatantly topless goddess. So the answer to "Why topless?" in the Cretan and Egyptian cases would seem to be: because Astarte/Isis ought to be depicted that way.

However, that still leaves unanswered the question of why the Canaanite Astarte should be topless. Endowing the new goddess Astarte with the age-old role of a fertility goddess would have effectively inserted her into the prevailing pantheon while ensuring that the critical function of fertility was performed by a major goddess. While Venus was destined

---

[74] Velikovsky, p. 185

for a long career as the goddess of love, the earliest sources on Astarte/Ishtar depict her rather as a terrifying goddess, and some peoples took Venus as their goddess of war.

Meanwhile, in Greece, according to Velikovsky, planet Venus was originally named Athena. But where did Athena get her name, and what did it mean?

A Fena

Many visitors to the Greek volcanic island Santorini have noted the curious fact that the Greek name of the island—Thira—differs only slightly from the name of its main town—Fira. We can surmise that the locals are still pronouncing the name in the original way for the town while uninformed outsiders have changed the F to Th for the island.

If we apply this pattern to Athena, her original name appears to be A Fena. Instead of the unpersuasive etymologies usually offered for Athena or the unsatisfactory solution of no etymology at all, A Fena is rich in meaning. It means The Phoenician, the perfect epithet for Venus, the brilliant comet arising as the Morning Star over Phoenicia. It also may have been deliberately chosen to link up with the cult of the great goddess Astarte/Ishtar from the Near East.

With the passage of time, outsiders evidently changed the F to Th, and as the name Athena spread throughout Greece, the link with Phoenicia and with the original meaning of Venus was lost. So the Greeks recruited a new goddess for Venus, which over the centuries was slowly losing its cometary tail and had ceased to approach and threaten Earth, instead becoming a benign beauty: Aphrodite.[75] Tellingly, Aphrodite's epithet in Homer was Kibris—Cyprus, also a place to the east where Venus rose every morning.

Thus the old argument of Martin Nilsson that the famous Minoan Snake Goddess was related to Athena receives significant support. And we can perceive that the Romans' Venus was originally Fenus, also The Phoenician. It is not clear whether Fenus was originally a male and then

---

[75] "Aphrodite" possibly originated thus: Astarte>Athtart>Aphtart>Aphrodite.

shifted gender, or whether the masculine ending of Venus, -us, most anomalous for the goddess of love, was actually an attempt to capture the S sound of the third consonant in FeNiS (Phoenician). The etymology typically provided for Venus—that it came from *venere*—would appear to have the direction reversed.

Poseidon

Meanwhile, Poseidon also plays a key role in this story. Before Poseidon was assigned the sea as his domain and given a trident, he had been quite different. His epithet of Earth Shaker has suggested to various scholars that he was a chthonic god, and this is traced back to a putative Central Asian origin, far from the sea. However, if we view Poseidon from the perspective of the Near East, a different pattern emerges.

With the common change of P to B, we have the Greek word for bull: *Bos*. And it is followed by *eidon*. In the Linear B Mycenaean Greek, this is variously rendered as *edao* or *edawone*. These variants can be seen as efforts by Greek speakers to capture the vowel sounds of the Semitic *eden* עדן, the word for paradise or heaven. Eventually the Greeks came to use ei (ει) for the Semitic ayin (ע). As the ayin in turn tended to lower or darken the second, unwritten vowel, they rendered that as omega (ω), yielding Poseidon (Ποσειδων). In other words, we are dealing with *Bos-eden (*pronounced more like *Bos-eidon)*, the Bull of Heaven, with the Greeks taking over the Semitic word for heaven, perhaps in imitation of what the Minoans had originally done (the Minoans may also have been the first to use the epithet The Phoenician).

This interpretation of the name Poseidon fits closely with the well-known bull cult of Minoan Crete as well as with the later Greek myth of Poseidon as the instigator of the Minotaur. Poseidon was also the deity of bull cults in Crete and elsewhere in Greece. In effect, the Minoans, and the Mycenaeans after them, had both male and female (The Snake Goddess) gods for the comet-planet Venus. And the epithet "Earth Shaker" of Poseidon is not an indicator of a chthonic god, but rather entirely comprehensible as the epithet of a Venus god whose close approaches to Earth occasioned devastating earthquakes via gravitational interaction.

The ancient peoples had no desire to offend the Bull of Heaven. However, they would also have liked to obtain protection against him. Thus we read in *The Epic of Gilgamesh* of the heroic slaying of the Bull of Heaven. And perhaps this can also explain the remarkable Master Impression of Chania (Kydonia) from Minoan times.

In Figure 21, the only object to be seen in the sky is at the right, behind the Master. It is a puffy, 3-lobed cloud (hard to explain) with two prongs extending upward from it (easy to explain—the twin tails of Venus, aka the horns of the Bull of Heaven). One interpretation would be that the Master was the Minoan equivalent of an evolved Poseidon, a powerful figure associated with the bull cult but capable of using his long spear to protect his people by slaying the Bull of Heaven. If this didn't work out, the so-called "horns of consecration" on the houses perhaps could serve to placate the Bull of Heaven, even as they honored the Minoan version of Poseidon. The Master has horns, and his hair divides into two trailing sets of strands.

Figure 21. Master Impression of Chania (Kydonia)

All this leaves us in a position better to interpret the famous mythical contest between Athena and Poseidon for the favor of the Athenian people—the right to be the patron deity of the city. In a sense, it was an effort to decide about the comet-planet—Is it a boy or is it a girl? The decision in favor of Athena was hedged by a cautious retention of the traditional ceremonies of the Erechthion, the most sacred of Athenian places and associated with Poseidon. One did not want to offend such a powerful god. Who, after all, had caused the explosion of Santorini and repeated massive earthquakes? Not for nothing was he called the Earth Shaker.

Chapter 8

Catastrophes and Climate Change in Ancient China

Immanuel Velikovsky referred repeatedly to Chinese evidence to buttress his arguments. But *Worlds in Collision* was never translated into Chinese, while the controversy over his Venus and Reversing Earth theories appears to have had little resonance in China itself. Also, new evidence and interpretation regarding both ancient China and the theories have appeared since 1950.[76]

The Chinese geological and archaeological literature contain many references to "marine transgressions". It is said that the coastline was pushed as much as 100 km to the west.[77] In all likelihood, some of these transgressions were not merely instances of hard-to-explain high sea levels, but rather were the consequences of enormous tsunamis during the inversions of ca 2200, 1628, 1210, and 820 BC. These tsunamis (or

---

[76] For a fuller account that includes Chinese sources, see Kenneth J. Dillon and Miao Li, "Catastrophes and Climate Change in Ancient China" at http://www.scientiapress.com/catastrophes-and-climate-change-in-ancient-china.

[77] Gideon Shelach-Lavi, *The Archaeology of Early China: From Prehistory to the Han Dynasty* (New York: Cambridge University Press, 2015), 166; Li Liu, *The Chinese Neolithic: Trajectories to Early States* (Cambridge: Cambridge University Press, 2004), 197

possibly just that of 2200 BC) flooded at least as far as the Shang capital Anyang, hundreds of kilometers from the present coastline, if the discovery of the remains of a whale near Anyang is any indication.[78]

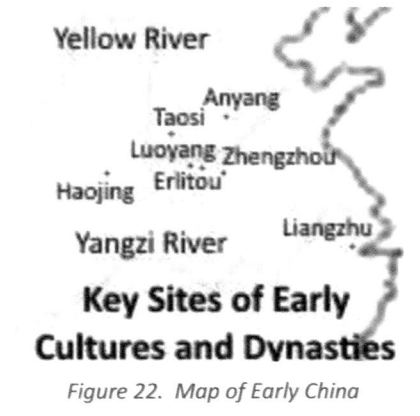

Yellow River

Anyang
Taosi
Luoyang Zhengzhou
Haojing Erlitou
Yangzi River   Liangzhu

Key Sites of Early Cultures and Dynasties

Figure 22. Map of Early China

The ca 2200 BC tsunami seems to have utterly destroyed the Liangzhu Culture in the Yangzi Delta region, leaving the area swamped for decades.[79] It devastated the Longshan Culture of north-central China as well. The archaeological sites dated to the succeeding Yueshi and Erlitou (Xia) cultures number only 14 and 20 percent of the Longshan sites, respectively.[80] Not only was there terrible loss of life. The advanced Neolithic culture of Liangzhu was replaced only after several hundred years by the much less sophisticated Maqiao culture, so abundant knowledge, skills, and property, including livestock, were lost.[81] Thus China's flood myths were based on historical reality, and the floods were not caused by excessive rainfall and river flows.

Still, the characteristics of these tsunamis require elucidation. How high were they when they hit the coastline? How far inland did they penetrate? How much water did they contain? Did they in fact take many years to drain away from China's interior, as the myths suggest? How did they differ from typical seaquake-induced tsunamis? Were there indeed four? Were they all roughly equal in size, or did the first and third one, coming across the Pacific, far surpass the second and fourth, coming from the Pacific as well, but on an inverted Earth and so perhaps significantly smaller?

---

[78] K.C. Chang, *The Archaeology of Ancient China*, 4th ed. (New Haven: Yale University Press, 1987), 139
[79] Shelach-Lavi, 166
[80] Liu, 31
[81] D.J. Stanley, Chen Zhongyuan, and Song Jian, "Inundation, Sea Level Rise and Transition from Neolithic to Bronze Age Cultures, Yangzi Delta, China," *Geoarchaeology* 14(1) (1999): 15-26

More evidence from China can help in answering these questions. For instance, a hunt for the remains of whales and other sea creatures in the interior of China might show how far the floods penetrated. But much of the evidence needed to characterize the tsunamis will have to come from investigations around the entire world.

The floods, along with the accompanying earthquakes and volcanic eruptions caused by close approaches of Venus, drastically affected the political and social systems of the Chinese dynasties. A working hypothesis can assume that the tsunamis played a key role in undermining the various dynasties, though collapse and replacement might have required many decades or even a century or two. Thus Longshan Culture, perhaps the Yü dynasty mentioned in Chinese texts,[82] collapsed in the aftermath of the ca 2200 BC catastrophe. The Xia dynasty collapsed following the ca 1628 BC catastrophe. Shang collapsed following the ca 1210 BC catastrophe. And the Western Zhou dynasty's unified power disintegrated following the ca 820 BC catastrophe.

While it is true that the capitals of the Xia and Western Zhou dynasties were in the west, the references in texts associating them with the west might alternatively be interpreted as alluding to the post-inversion rise of the Sun and Venus in the west during their sways. Similarly, Shang was associated with the east, and the Sun presumably arose in the east both during Longshan and the post-Western Zhou era.

Dynasty	Dates BC	Inversion BC	Key Site	Sun/Venus rose in the
Longshan/Yü?	3000-2000	2200		east
Xia	1970-1600	1628	Taosi/Erlitou	west
Shang	1600-1046	1210	Zhengzhou/Anyang	east
Western Zhou	1045-771	820	Haojing/Luoyang	west
Eastern Zhou	770-250	None	Various	east

Figure 23. Chinese Dynasties and Inversions

---

[82] Bernhard Karlgren, "Legends and Cults in Ancient China," *Bulletin of the Museum of Far Eastern Antiquities*, No. 18 (1946): 199-365, pp. 217-8

Climate Change

Since Venus and Earth interacted perhaps 32 times on a 52-year cycle, and each interaction involved at least a small gravitational tug on Earth that would displace its body in a minor or occasionally major way, there were actually many climate changes. And some would have cancelled each other out. Also, the interactions caused perturbations in Earth's orbit that affected the amount of insolation, while the dust from volcanoes triggered around the world tended to cool the climate.

After 3000 BC a minor cooling trend abruptly sharpened around 2500 BC, soon after Venus began to interact with the Earth. The climate is also generally thought to have become drier, yet one view is that precipitation actually increased.[83] Then, around 2200 BC, a catastrophic event (the global 4.2 ka event, the first inversion) devastated Longshan and destroyed Liangzhu.

A colder, drier climate seems to have characterized the Xia dynasty era from 1970 BC onward. Then there was a second inversion around 1628 BC. It must have set off a tsunami, but the evidence that this putative tsunami was as thoroughly destructive as the first one is lacking. The shift to the Shang dynasty was accompanied, it seems, by a warming trend that made the temperature in Northern China perhaps 2°C warmer than present-day temperature. In turn, the inversion around 1210 BC, which led ultimately to the overthrow of Shang by the Western Zhou dynasty around 1046 BC, appears to have completely swept away the people and culture of the Yangzi Delta region, just as had happened 1000 years before with Liangzhu but had apparently not happened at the time of the second inversion around 1628 BC.[84] This suggests that this tsunami of circa 1210

---

[83] Tracey L.D. Lu, "Mid-Holocene climate and cultural dynamics in eastern Central China," in: *Climate Change and Cultural Dynamics: A Global Perspective on Mid-Holocene Transitions*. David G. Anderson *et al.*, eds. (Amsterdam: Academic Press, 2007), 297

[84] Shiyong Yu *et al.*, "Role of climate in the rise and fall of Neolithic cultures on the Yangtze Delta," *Boreas* 29 (2000): 157-65, p. 157. These researchers write that "the civilization in the region terminated mysteriously" around 3000 BP, which can be taken to refer to roughly 1210 BC.

BC was of the magnitude of the first tsunami, and both were larger than the putative tsunami of 1628 BC.

During the Western Zhou period, some evidence suggests that the climate became colder than during Shang or in the present day. The *Bamboo Annals* report that at various times the Han and Hangzi Rivers froze. A major drought occurred, and the Jing, Wei, and Luo Rivers ran dry.[85] Yet the presence of bamboo and plum in Northern China, plus possible double-cropping, suggests that during the Western Zhou era temperatures were warmer than today's.[86] Finally, there is no evidence that the putative tsunami connected with the inversion of 820 BC was of the magnitude of the tsunamis associated with the first and third inversions.

Three patterns emerge from this account. First, the climate changes in China that occurred between 2550 and 800 BC were consistent with the suggested pattern of inversions and tsunamis in other places, but they were more complicated, presumably because the approaches of Venus every 52 years caused minor changes in the orientation of the Earth's body and thereby the climate. Another factor might have been a shift from an initial disruption immediately following an inversion to an adjustment to a more benign long-term climatic regime. Second, the climate during "upright" phases when the Sun rose in the east (before 2200 BC, during Shang, and after 820 BC) was generally but not always warmer, while the "inverted" phases when the Sun rose in the west (Xia and Western Zhou) had generally colder and drier climates. Third, the first and third inversions were of a much greater magnitude than the second and fourth ones.

Impact and Response

China's rulers responded to the catastrophes by commanding scholars and subordinates to map out the new situations with new calendars and

---

[85] Michael Loewe and Edward L. Shaughnessy, eds., *The Cambridge History of Ancient China: From the Origins of Civilization to 221 BC* (Cambridge: Cambridge University Press, 1999), 35
[86] Ibid.

new designations of directions. Thus, Emperor Yao "commanded the Hsis and Hos, in reverent accordance with the wide heavens, to calculate and delineate the sun, the moon, the stars, and the zodiacal spaces, and so to deliver respectfully the seasons to be observed by the people." Yao went on to dispatch scholars to east, south, west, and north in order to establish the seasons according to the heavens and for the use of the people.[87] Xia, Shang, and Zhou each re-established directional order and created a new calendar following the catastrophes.[88]

Myths transformed the Yellow Emperor into a super-human, but we can see that originally he was Venus and that his battles referred in part to the encounters of Venus with Mars, in one case termed the Flame Emperor (*Yandi*) and in another case *Chi You*. The best explanation of battles against two variants of Mars is that Venus and Mars interacted on more than one occasion, and the Chinese myth makers threaded these interactions into their accounts of actual earthly combats. Thus in a parallel to the *Iliad*'s simultaneous celestial and terrestrial battles between Greeks backed by Athena (Venus) and Trojans backed by Ares (Mars), the Huaxia led by *Huangdi* (Venus) fought the Jiuli (including the Miao) led by *Chi You* (Mars).

The pattern of human sacrifices to Venus elsewhere in the world suggests that the increase in Longshan and the very high numbers in Shang were to propitiate Venus. In some cases these human sacrifices were for the ancestors, presumably either to induce them to intercede with Venus or to ensure that they were not somehow offended and therefore unleashing destruction. In other cases, the human sacrifices may have been directly offered to Venus.

The astronomical observatory at Taosi in Shanxi, variously assigned dates ending between 2100 and 1900 BC, has been interpreted as a solar observatory.[89] However, many alignments make no sense for tracking the

---

[87] William Legge, trans., *The Shu King, the Canon of Yao* (London, 1879), 32 ff; Velikovsky, 115
[88] Lewis, 30; Loewe and Shaughnessy, 19-20
[89] David W. Pankanier, *Astrology and Cosmology in Early China: Conforming Earth to Heaven* (New York: Cambridge University Press, 2013); David W. Pankenier, Ciyuan Y. Liu, and Salvo De Meis, "The Xiangfen, Taosi Site: A Chinese Neolithic 'Observatory'," *Archaeologia Baltica* 10 (2009): 141-7; Wu Jiabi, Chen Meidong,

rising Sun in the east, and after 2200 BC the Sun was rising in the west anyway! The alignments on both ends of the curving row in the site extend well beyond solstice points and can better be interpreted as tracking the Evening Star/Comet as it set in the east. Thus the Taosi site can be interpreted as primarily a Venus observatory. As such, it would have served as the ideal setting for human sacrifices to Venus (though there is little evidence of them).[90] This would also fit with the powerful needs to track the whereabouts of Venus as a threat and an omen—e.g., of war. Venus was a war god. According to *Huainanzi* 3:7b:5, "When (Venus) should appear but does not appear, or should not yet disappear but does disappear, throughout the world armies will be withdrawn. When Venus should disappear but does not disappear or should not yet appear but does appear, throughout the world armies will set forth."[91]

Chinese Myths

Venus' large body blocked sunlight from the central portion of its cometary tail, leaving two long, bright streaks on the sides. As discussed in Chapter 4, in China, the curve of the body of Venus and the two streaks were seen as a bow. Thus the mythical Archer Yi with his vermilion bow was Venus. While one version of the myth had Yi shoot down nine of ten suns appearing simultaneously in the sky because they made the Earth too hot, a vigorous competing version spoke of ten successive suns.[92] In

---

and Liu Ciyuan, "Astronomical function and date of the Taosi observatory," *Science in China Series G: Physics, Mechanics & Astronomy* 52/1 (2009): 151-8; Li, 323

[90] Some human sacrifice remains have been found in the foundation of an adjacent building. He Nu, "The Longshan Period Site of Taosi in Southern Shanxi Province" in: Anne P. Underhill, ed., *A Companion to Chinese Archaeology* (New York: Wiley, 2013), 255-77, p. 267. For a parallel, see Ivan Ghezzi and Clive Ruggles, "Chankillo: A 2300-Year Old Solar Observatory in Coastal Peru," *Science* 315 (2 March 2007): 1239-43.

[91] John S. Major, *Heaven and Earth in Early Han Thought: Chapters Three, Four, and Five of the* Huainanzi (Albany: SUNY Press, 1993), 76

[92] Allan, 26

effect, as the Sun followed a different track across the sky on each day of an inversion, Yi's bow, directed by the solar wind, tracked the new sun. The ten suns were reported as an ill omen at the ends of the Xia dynasty (*Bamboo Annals*) and of the Shang dynasty (*Huainanzi*, 15/6b).[93] Over time, Archer Yi, who began in the east, became identified with the west as well,[94] presumably because Venus and the Sun rose in the west.

Venus was yellow when it first appeared in the skies over China, hence the name Yellow Emperor, with his human face and dragon tail. Then it turned red as interplanetary dust and dust rising from catastrophes on Earth obscured vision: the Vermilion Bird, the Red Pearl, etc.

In another myth, the Jingwei bird tirelessly carried wood and stones from the western mountains to build a dike against the Eastern Sea.[95] This is a rare specific reference to floods being caused by transgressions resulting (we must assume) from tsunamis.

Lastly, we have the myth of Gong Gong: "Anciently Gong Gong and Zhuan Xu fought, each seeking to become the Thearch (Emperor). Enraged, they crash against Mt. Buzhou; Heaven's pillars broke, the cords of Earth snapped. Heaven tilted in the northwest, and thus the sun and moon, stars and planets shifted in that direction. Earth became unfull in the southeast, and thus the watery floods and mounding soils subsided in that direction." (*Huainanzi* 3:1a:1.)[96] This seems to refer to a displacement of Earth's body resulting from an encounter with Venus. While perhaps only a small change in latitude, not a 180° inversion, such a displacement could affect climate to an extent that would rival the change caused by an inversion, thus complicating the effort to specify the dates and distinctiveness of inversions. Such displacements might also account for the departures from true north in the alignments of Xia and Shang buildings. Those at Erlitou (Xia) were oriented 6-10° west of present-day north; those at Shang sites were oriented 7° east of present-day north.[97]

---

[93] Ibid., 38
[94] Ibid., 37
[95] Lewis, 10
[96] Major, 62
[97] Li Feng, *Early China. A Social and Cultural History* (Cambridge: Cambridge University Press, 2013), 60; Pankanier, 2013, 119-22

Venus and Mars were depicted as dragons because of their cometary tails (in Mars' case, borrowed from Venus). Dragon combats became a perennial art genre. The popular imagination spread the notion to include sea serpents and sea horses, some of which presumably had been swept inland by the tsunamis. Thus the proliferation of dragons in imagery, the depiction of sages with human heads and dragon tails, and possibly the belief that seahorses have special potency entered Chinese culture. One example is the imperial flag of the Qing dynasty, which has a dragon with a red ball (presumably Venus) in front of its mouth and twin streamers on the front that were originally the twin tails of the ball/Venus, though over time they became unhitched and instead connected to the dragon's mouth.

Conclusion

Clearly, Chinese evidence provides valuable corroboration of scenarios elsewhere in the world, just as findings from the rest of the world can help to elucidate the Chinese events.

The Chinese accounts help us see what Velikovsky termed cultural amnesia at work. We can readily understand that, following the end of the catastrophes, ancient Chinese writers would have been adamant about screening out accounts of the Sun and Venus rising in the west as contrary to reason and thus demonstrably false. Dread of Venus and efforts to propitiate it, moreover, made no sense at a time when Venus had lost most of its tail in encounters with Earth and Mars, had ceased to approach Earth, and had become the benign companion of the Sun. In addition, evidence that survived their filtering was reshaped to fit their preconceptions, as in the Daoist reworking of the Yellow Emperor myth and in the story of Archer Yi and the ten suns. The Archer Yi myth has double value, as a splendid depiction of the stunning phenomenon of a ten-day inversion, and, with its popular but incorrect version, as a perfect instance of cultural amnesia caught in the act. As we will note in the concluding chapter, Archer Yi is also Exhibit A in the case for using myth as a source of insight into history and science. Ancient peoples at times used myths to convey important knowledge.

With their shared uniformitarian outlook, cultural amnesia and Scientific Rejectionism constitute a tacit alliance determined to fight the Venus and Reversing Earth theories. But in vain. From the Chinese evidence, we can see major patterns substantiate the theories: the fit between the dynastic chronology and the approximate dates of inversions, paralleling the fit with Egypt's dynastic chronology; the evidence on the tsunami-caused floods; the correct interpretation of the correct version of the Archer Yi myth; and striking matches to evidence elsewhere in the world.

Chapter 9

Venus, Skeleton Key to Stonehenge

One of the world's most famous monuments, Stonehenge abounds in mysteries and anomalies.

Why was Stonehenge built in the first place? Why was it radically transformed shortly before 2500 BC into a masterpiece of megalithic architecture? What explains the intricate, changing patterns of the stones over time? Why the extraordinary effort?

The Venus theory provides answers to these and other questions.

Various pieces of evidence suggest that Stonehenge began its career around 3000 BC as a combined solar and lunar site. It also came to serve as a place of interment of cremated remains. The centerline of the northeastern entrance had a declination of +27°, close to that of the major lunar standstill.[98] Meanwhile, even though various suggestions for how the ring of 56 Aubrey Holes could have served to predict eclipses have not been widely accepted, the Holes remain suggestive of some kind of method for predicting eclipses, and thus Stonehenge would have been both a solar and a lunar site. Keeping a balance between gods seems to have

---

[98] See other arguments for a lunar use of the site in Clive Ruggles, "Astronomy and Stonehenge," *Proceedings of the British Academy* 92 (1997): 203-229.

been important to the people who ran Stonehenge, the principle being to avoid neglecting either deity because that could bring trouble.

When Comet Venus first approached Earth, around 2525 BC, gravitational interaction had dramatic consequences, in all probability including volcanic eruptions that generated atmospheric dust, earthquakes, and floods. The awesome appearance of Comet Venus and the accompanying devastation evidently inspired fear in peoples worldwide. Kings, chieftains, and shamans, whose credibility was at stake, responded by building sites and adapting existing ones to track Venus and also to propitiate the terrifying new god. These sites typically contained a Venus effigy that the comet god could see as he/she passed overhead: a serpent, a bull, a lion, or a bird.

Still others thought in terms of geometry. If the Sun was a circle and the Moon a crescent, the new comet-planet became an oval. Many sites, especially mounds, appear to have had stone, wooden, or earthen ovals on top of them where rituals were conducted; over time these ovals often transitioned into circles and rectangles. Silbury Hill north of Stonehenge is a circular mound, perhaps with an originally oval top, erected around 2500 BC at enormous effort, most likely for tracking Venus, worshipping it, and providing refuge in the event of a mega-tsunami.

Stonehenge's Greatest Phase

In response to Venus' first approach, the ruler of the Stonehenge region arranged for bluestones to be shipped from Wales (alternatively, collected from nearby glacial erratics), had giant sarsens (sandstones) hauled to the site, and ordered a stone monument constructed to replace the existing one, presumably largely or wholly wooden.

In keeping with the earlier practice of balancing the Sun and Moon, the builders sought to keep a balance between the fearsome new comet god and the mighty traditional ones. They expanded the northeastern entrance southward to ensure that the Sun's rays at summer solstice sunrise would reach the center of the site.

The builders designed a circle of sarsens with lintels that in effect declared allegiance to the Sun, which would explain their effort to achieve a perfectly level surface: only the best for the great Sun god. They used tenon-and-mortise joints to set the lintels atop the upright sarsens, and tong-and-groove joints to link the lintels, not merely following the practice of woodworkers, but rather to create an unusually stable ring that could resist earthquakes when Venus approached again. They gave the trilithon sarsens deep foundations for the same reason.[99]

Using the geometry of a diffraction grating,[100] the builders arranged the tall sarsens of the Trilithon Horseshoe symmetrically around the main northeast-southwest axis in an arc to represent the arc formed by Comet Venus' body and twin tails. As we have seen, a parallel arc concept is found in the original version of the Chinese myth of Archer Yi and his vermilion bow that targeted (shifting with the solar wind) the ten suns that appeared on successive days (as Earth inverted), sparing the tenth one.

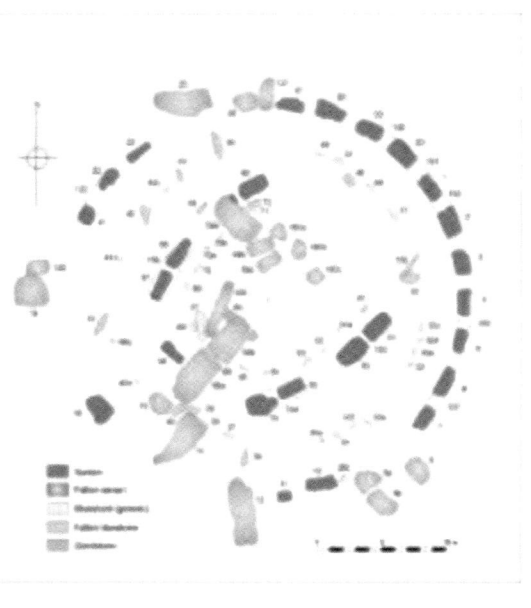

Figure 24. Stonehenge ca 2500 BC

There are reasons to think that the Stonehenge site was oriented primarily toward the southwest.[101] The flat, smooth side of the Great Trilithon stones, for instance, was turned to face southwest in order to salute the Evening Star, in contrast to the other stones, which faced

---

[99] Euan W. MacKie, "Megalithic Astronomy and Catastrophism," *Pensée*, Vol. 4, No. 5 (1974-75): 5-20
[100] Anthony Johnson, *Solving Stonehenge. The New Key to an Ancient Enigma* (London: Thames & Hudson, 2008), 244
[101] Christopher Chippindale, *Stonehenge Complete,* 4th ed. (London: Thames & Hudson, 2012), 236-7

inward. As had other peoples worldwide, Stonehenge's builders evidently recognized that the Morning Star posed no threat. It was the Evening Star that could disappear at Inferior Conjunction and approach Earth. Hence the need to monitor the Evening Star meticulously, especially at its greatest elongation, to ensure that it was on track and would not approach Earth. They also needed to make sure that the heliacal rising of the Morning Star occurred as expected after eight days of Inferior Conjunction; if it didn't, that could be a sign that Venus was approaching.

How Stonehenge was used to monitor Venus remains a topic for future research and must be considered in conjunction with the alignments of other megalithic monuments built in the period after ca 2525 BC.[102] The insertion of the four Station Stones at Stonehenge might have contributed to such monitoring because they would have assisted in tracking the setting of the Evening Star to the northwest around summer solstice.

In spite of the focus on the Evening Star that the size and geometry of the Trilithon Horseshoe indicate, the builders' apparent concern for balance suggests that the orientation of the Great Trilithon toward the southwest was also intended to honor the setting winter solstice Sun. Thus Stonehenge appears to have served as a site where processions along the Avenue from the River Avon approached the site at winter solstice dusk to honor the setting Sun and the Evening Star in the southwest, and at summer solstice dawn to honor the Sun and the Morning Star in the northeast.

For the sake of comparison, the wooden southern circle at nearby Durrington Walls, with a horseshoe array, is thought to have been the lodging place of the Stonehenge workers, entered from an avenue from the river on the southeast. Its main orientation was northwest,[103] which would have been useful for tracking the setting Evening Star at its greatest elongation around summer solstice, while also honoring the setting Sun at summer solstice. Nearby Woodhenge ring was in the shape of an oval.

---

[102] The alignment of stones at Ballochroy in Scotland, for instance, has been viewed as intended to track the summer solstice sunset but may have primarily been meant to track the setting of the Evening Star at its greatest elongation.

[103] Mike Parker Pearson and the Stonehenge Riverside Project, *Stonehenge. A New Understanding* (New York: The Experiment, 2013), 91

The First and Second Inversions

The pristine megalithic configuration of Stonehenge remained intact from ca 2525 to ca 2200 BC.

But every 52 years Venus approached again, causing disruptions that set off migrations of peoples, including that of the Beaker Ware people from the Continent around 2400 BC. In addition, certain approaches of Venus seem to have caused Earth's body to move slightly, complicating the problem of determining possible alignments, as if the shifting and settling of stones over time had not made it sufficiently difficult.

An especially close approach of Venus ca 2200 (the 4.2 ka event) caused the first inversion, accompanied by volcanic eruptions, earthquakes, and perhaps floods. Now the Sun, Moon, Venus, and stars moved from west to east. That meant that the Evening Star's furthest elongation could be tracked in the northeast, and the Evening Star could be monitored in the southeast as well. This might explain the three post holes discovered in the southeastern side of the bank[104] that are in respect to the center of the Aubrey Holes ring at a declination limit of -28°, close to the purported -27° declination limit of Venus for 2500-1500 BC.[105] In fact, given the somewhat irregular and more elliptical orbit of ancient Venus than its orbit today, it is possible that the Evening Star at greatest elongation was on a slightly more eccentric orbit, and thus a -28° declination limit might have been exactly right. We also must ask if changes made at the northeastern entrance were intended to facilitate monitoring of Venus.

---

[104] Ruggles, "Astronomy and Stonehenge," 218
[105] Ibid., 210

In response to the first inversion, the Beaker people, though more expert at metalworking, than at stone construction, appear to have felt a need to upgrade Stonehenge's capacity for communicating with Venus. After all, the existing configuration had failed to prevent the catastrophic inversion, perhaps because Venus did not understand the arc pattern formed by the Trilithon Horseshoe. So they built a bluestone oval[106] inside the Trilithon Horseshoe to make sure that Venus saw the oval and arc, and recognized their loyalty.

The Sun, for its part, had played a mysterious role and followed an astounding trajectory during the inversion. Now it amazingly rose in the west. Therefore, to maintain balance with Venus and to honor the mighty, wondrous western-rising Sun, the Beaker people set up a bluestone circle outside the Trilithon Horseshoe. Mindful that the Moon also was transformed into a marvelous western-rising version, we must wonder whether Stonehenge's owners might have found some way to honor the translocated Moon in the new configuration

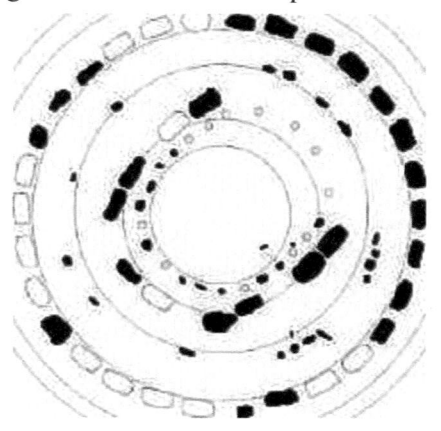

Figure 25. Stonehenge after the ca 2200 Inversion

The ensuing epoch saw the high tide of the metalworking Wessex Culture. Stonehenge appears to have been in constant use. Then "quite suddenly, or so it seems, something happened to disrupt the established order."[107] That something was the second inversion ca 1628 BC. After an unsuccessful attempt ca 1600 BC to build two more rings (the X and Y Holes), Stonehenge was abandoned, possibly in part because it had suffered damage from the inversion catastrophe.

Over time Venus changed, too. It slowly lost its ovoid shape. Its giant tail diminished from encounters with Earth and Mars. After the third and

---

[106] Timothy Darvill *et al.*, "Stonehenge remodeled," *Antiquity* 86 (2012): 1021-1040, pp. 1036-7
[107] Johnson, 33

fourth inversions, it became simply a beautiful star, considered an evermore subordinate companion to the Sun.

Conclusion

Comprehending the role of Venus in archaeoastronomy and the Bronze Age catastrophes can help explain both the chronology of megalithic Stonehenge and the complex, changing patterns of its stones. Driven by fear and awe, and employing geometric patterns in masterful stonework, the ancient people who built and used Stonehenge were engaged in a dead serious effort to communicate with and show reverence for the gods in the sky above, in particular the terrifying Comet Venus.

Chapter 10

Venus in the Americas

Since the approaches of Venus began shortly before 2500 BC, in the Mesoamerican context most of the first 1000 years of Venus' dramatic interactions with Earth took place before the rise of the Olmecs, the first civilized people in the region. Thus both the scanty pre-Olmec evidence, e.g., in early mounds, and Olmec culture as the first articulated repository of Mesoamerican knowledge gain special relevance because their sources were eyewitnesses to the arrival of Venus and the first catastrophes.

The inversions of ca 2200, 1628, 1210, and 820 BC caused the overwhelming catastrophes associated with the ends of suns or world ages in Mayan and Aztec accounts. Subinversional events also occurred on not-so-close encounters between Venus and Earth on a 52-year cycle. They may have dislodged Earth's body by several degrees and could explain otherwise odd orientations of buildings and cities.

Our possession of an approximate chronology of inversions can help us detect alignments and references to the western-rising Sun in Mesoamerican literature and iconography. However, the fact that the last inversion occurred around 820 BC also tells us that the great preponderance of astronomical evidence we possess—from Teotihuacan, Toltecs, Mayans, and Aztecs—is not contemporaneous with the catastrophes. Thus it was vulnerable to erosion and reshaping by cultural amnesia. Still, in a remarkable irony, Mesoamerican civilization faithfully and tenaciously retained the most highly detailed records of the astronomy and practices associated with Venus and the catastrophes of any civilization.

We now know that in ancient times Venus was an ovoid, though it slowly turned into a spheroid. Certain depictions of Venus in glyphs contain ovals, and we can hunt for oval mounds. The Pyramid of the Magician in Uxmal has an oval base reminiscent of oval temples in Mesopotamia. Mindful of the power of cultural amnesia, we can ask whether circular patterns in buildings associated with Venus[108] or in the widespread small pecked-cross circles were originally oval.[109] Because an oval can be reshaped into a rectangle, we could hunt beneath rectangles to find evidence of this, particularly in mounds.

We now better understand the role of effigy monuments in the responses of people worldwide to the awesome and fearsome Comet Venus. They felt a powerful urge to propitiate the god, and they did so via effigies and sacrifices. The surmise that the great Olmec mound in San

---

[108] "A number of early chronicles link round structures to a cult connected with Quetzalcoatl-Kukulcan [Venus]....", Susan Milbrath, *Star Gods of the Maya: Astronomy in Art, Folklore, and Calendars* (Austin: University of Texas Press, 1999), 177. The attribution of westward-oriented buildings to the Evening Star and eastward-oriented ones to the Morning Star (pp. 177-8) seems less than persuasive. Arguably, all observatory buildings were pointed toward the setting of the Evening Star because it was considered more dangerous and thus required meticulous monitoring, but this meant the east at the time of a western-rising Sun because that is where Venus set.

[109] An early one pecked on the floor of Structure A-V in Uaxactun, Guatemala seems ovoid: Anthony F. Aveni. *Skywatchers* (Austin: University of Texas Press, 2001), 330, fig 126h. However, the camera angle might make a circle appear oval. Fig 126c on p. 330 shows a circular pecked cross with a curling, serpent-like tail. There is an oval outer ring surrounding the pecked cross on Fig 54.1b on p. 739 of Stanislaw Iwaniszewski, "Pecked Cross Circles", in: Ruggles: 737-42. Over time, as the collapse of the Sun became more feared than Venus and as Venus became spheroidal, the shape of the pecked-cross circles became circular, perhaps to denote the Sun.

Lorenzo was a giant bird effigy[110] neatly fits into this pattern, and other such effigies may still exist, as yet undiscovered, in Mesoamerica.

The Original Theory Explains Much

In its original version, Velikovsky's Venus theory nicely explains many Mesoamerican phenomena. Comet Venus as the Morning Star was Quetzalcoatl, the plumed serpent. Venus was also called the Red Star because interplanetary and atmospheric dust stirred up by the catastrophes made it look red. The mythical battles of Quetzalcoatl with Tezcatlipoca were accounts of the interaction of Venus and Mars, as in the *Iliad* and in Chinese myths. Over time Venus lost its cometary tail in encounters with Earth and Mars. As its orbit circularized from repeated tugs of Earth's and Mars' gravity and other factors, and particularly after the last inversion ca 820 BC, Venus added to its original identity as a war god, demanding bloody sacrifices, a very different identity as the Rain God Chac/Tlaloc, in keeping with its appearance coinciding with the rainy season. Of course, the malign/benign dualism derived as well from the distinction between Evening Star and Morning Star.

Velikovsky also correctly interpreted the Mayan and Aztec accounts of the ends of four worlds to fit the four inversions. We should also note that the inversions suggested that the Sun itself could be a source of danger (that it would collapse) and thus required human hearts and blood. This would explain why ritual human sacrifices shifted from being offered to the ever-more-benign Venus, whose movements were becoming more predictable and less threatening, to being directed to the Sun, in an effort to ensure that the Fifth Sun, our present era in Aztec lore, would not also end in catastrophe.

Scholars have found that the Aztecs misnamed the Pyramid of the Sun at Teotihuacan. Possibly they misnamed the Pyramid of the Moon as well. If so, the pyramids may both have been monuments to various aspects of

---

[110] R.M. Rosenswig and R.L. Burger, eds., *Early New World Monumentality* (Gainesville: University of Florida, 2012), 299, citing Michael D. Coe and Richard A. Diehl, *In the Land of the Olmec* (Austin: University of Texas Press, 1980)

Tlaloc/Venus. Thus, including the Temple of Quetzalcoatl (the Morning Star), Teotihuacan was a largely or wholly Venus site.

We can also interpret the well-known ball game of Mesoamerica as a contest to bet on/influence the possibility of a new inversion of the Sun that would shift its rising from east to west, or vice versa. Of course, many variants of the ball game existed, and there were many purposes for which they were played.

Velikovsky pointed out that the observational "mistakes" in Mesoamerican and other ancient records of Venus were actually accurate. During the Bronze Age Catastrophes, Venus had an irregular and hard-to-track orbit that deviated from the present-day pattern.[111] In turn, this explains why the Mesoamericans were so eager to monitor its orbit: when Venus disappeared, especially at Inferior Conjunction, it could be approaching Earth. Hence the malign character of the Evening Star, which was the one that might approach; the need to follow it carefully at its greatest elongation; the sacred significance of the number 8 as the normal length in days of the Inferior Conjunction; and the fear attending the date of the hoped-for heliacal rising of the Morning Sun as well as the joy when it rose as hoped.

Mesoamerica in Venus Theory Research

Four conclusions suggest themselves.

First, *Worlds in Collision* should be translated into Spanish.

Second, students of Mesoamerican archaeoastronomy need to familiarize themselves with *Worlds in Collision* and the new findings and reinterpretations regarding the Venus theory.

Third, we need to reexamine many phenomena in Mesoamerican history and culture in the light of the revised and enhanced Venus theory. For instance, the theory offers opportunities for better defining and explaining orientations, yet at the same time it complicates the issue,

---

[111] Livio C. Stecchini, "Astronomical Theory and Historical Data," in: Alfred de Grazia, ed., *The Velikovsky Affair. The Warfare of Science and Scientism* (New Hyde Park NY: University Books, 1966): 146 ff

because one must ask whether the era in which the orientation was established was one of a western-rising Sun, or whether the orientation followed the practice of such an era even after it ended. Similarly, dislocations of Earth's body during sub-inversions could affect orientations in a hard-to-ascertain manner. We also need to investigate the important role of Mars in the Venus theory.

Fourth, we need to exploit newly interpreted, rich Mesoamerican sources on Venus and archaeoastronomy to contribute to the correct interpretation of archaeoastronomy sites worldwide.

And now let us examine the most outstanding Venus site north of Mexico.

Great Serpent Mound Was an Effigy of Venus

The 420-meter long Great Serpent Mound in Ohio is the world's longest effigy monument. Archaeological investigations have yielded conflicting conjectures about its initial construction date, and various theories regarding its meaning have failed to gain traction. But a revised and enhanced version of the theory of Immanuel Velikovsky, that the planet Venus was originally a comet that approached the Earth and caused great devastation, neatly matches key characteristics of the Great Serpent Mound.

Figure 26. Great Serpent Mound

Why should we believe that the Great Serpent Mound was a depiction of the comet Venus before it was tamed by interaction with the Earth and Mars into a planet with a circular orbit and only the vestige of a tail?

1. Many peoples around the world viewed and depicted the comet Venus as a serpent god because of its tail.[112]
2. The setting of the Great Serpent Mound is a very ancient impact crater and thus was associated with celestial events such as the meteorites that fell from the tail of Venus.
3. The timing is approximately right. The original construction could have occurred at some time after the first approach of Venus just before 2500 BC, or soon after the great catastrophe of 2200 BC during a particularly close approach. These early dates were before Venus began gradually to turn more spheroid and lose its long, double tail. They precede the Adena culture, which began around 1200-1000 BC. Subsequent peoples would have refurbished the monument, accounting for some later radiocarbon-dated objects found in it.
4. The appearances and impact of Venus were dramatic, catastrophic, and repeated on a 52-year cycle, leading the builders to propitiate and venerate the god with a massive monument.
5. Building an effigy this size would help the Serpent God see it on future approaches to the Earth and hopefully spare his devoted worshippers who had constructed it.
6. The oval "egg" in front of the mouth of the serpent represents a molten, ovoid Comet Venus that had been elongated by Jupiter's gravitational pull on passing the gas giant and that proceeded along the direction of its longer axis like a bullet in its trajectory.
7. The comet Venus was far larger than other comets, and so its tail was bifurcated, with the central portion blacked out from solar illumination by the body of the comet/planet. As we have seen, this led it to be termed the "bull of heaven" by peoples of the Near East and the Greeks, who viewed the twin tails as the horns of a bull. In the Great Serpent Mound, the jaws of the serpent are opened in a manner that depicts how the portion immediately

---

[112] It seems, for instance, that the English geoglyph White Horse of Uffington was originally a depiction of a dragon/serpent Venus that over time became reconfigured as an elongated horse.

behind the oval ("egg") was blacked out, then the twin tails joined together as they trailed farther behind Venus. 19th-century observers also reported "Upon either side of the serpent's head extend two small triangular elevations, ten or twelve feet over. They are not high, and although too distinct to be overlooked, are yet too much obliterated to be satisfactorily traced."[113] The twin tails of Venus?

The Great Serpent Mound, in some ways the most outstanding ancient monument north of Mexico, thus provides an excellent match with the Venus theory.

This finding can help explain the long controversy over whether the Moundbuilders of pre-Columbian America were native Americans or whether they came from some exotic origin with superior technology (Hebrews, Babylonians, Atlantaeans, etc.). The Venus catastrophes devastated native American cultures that were in certain ways more advanced than those that replaced them and were encountered by European settlers. In other words, even though those observers who sought to identify an exotic source were mistaken, they may have been right to perceive a significant technological gap.

---

[113] Ephraim G. Squier and Edwin H. Davis, *Ancient Monuments of the Mississippi Valley* (Washington, D.C.: Smithsonian Institution Press, 1848, reprinted 1998), 13

Chapter 11

The Trojan Origin of Roman Civilization

Students have long struggled, often in vain, with the rules of Latin grammar. The structure of sentences in Latin seems strange to the mind of an Indo-European native speaker, as does Latin's heavy use of gerundive and absolute constructions. All those verbal nouns entail a very different pattern of thinking than goes on in modern Indo-European languages.

But in the eyes of a Hungarian or Turk, whose languages are rich in gerundive and absolute constructions, the grammar of classical Latin should seem oddly familiar. A sentence structure in which certain words are encapsulated within others in an order that confounds Indo-Europeans makes everyday sense (verbs in Germanic and Slavic languages form a partial exception). Yet Latin is the mother of the Romance languages and the *fons et origo* of grammatical studies in Europe.

An intriguing scenario might help explain this apparent paradox.

Some Greek writers held that the Etruscans were Trojans; and a great deal of myth, echoed by Vergil, claimed that Aeneas and other escapees from the destruction of Troy were the founders of Rome. Yet the Etruscans have come down in history as mysterious invaders from the east, or as autochthonous types (according to some scholars), whose language defies translation and seems related only to the remnants of Lemniac once spoken on the island of Lemnos.

Here is an explanation.

A Steppe People

Let us assume that Homer's "horse-taming" Trojans were a people who originated in the steppes north of the Black Sea and spoke a Ural-Altaic language similar to those in the modern world: Finno-Ugric languages, Turkic languages, Mongol, and Manchu, and their more distant cousins, Korean and Japanese. Around the year 1200 BC, perhaps in response to an earthquake that wrecked the walls of cities, the proto-Trojans moved south to settle on both banks of the strategic Straits leading from the Black Sea to the Mediterranean, conquering and intermingling with the local peoples. The Trojans possessed an instinct for domination and great military prowess—equal to the task of destroying the Hittite cities and the Mycenaean palaces, for which they must be considered the prime suspects, as well as becoming one of the Peoples of the Sea who attacked Egypt and eventually settled as the Philistines on the coast of Palestine.

To account for the complexity of Homer's *Iliad*, three main episodes seem warranted. The first would have been a pan-Hellenic Mycenaean expedition that conquered Ilion/Troy in the era preceding 1200 BC, leaving a rich array of Bronze Age detail in the oral epics that became the *Iliad* and *Odyssey*.

The second would have been the descent into the Aegean world around 1200 BC of the steppe nomads who became known as the Trojans and who proceeded to conquer Ilion.

The third episode would have been a second pan-Hellenic Iron Age conquest of Ilion, this time around 900 BC. Perhaps this was the archaeological Troy VIIA.

Homer evidently conflated the late Bronze Age and early Iron Age Greek expeditions against Ilion.

Following their conquest of the Straits region, the Trojans would have intermingled genetically with the peoples they subjected, picking up some local vocabulary and customs as well. The Trojans' superior might gave them control of the trade through the Straits, either through attacking merchant ships or by levying tolls. Presumably, they also engaged in trade themselves and through it and war loot amassed the wealth that went into building the fortress city of Ilion that withstood a Greek siege for a long time. Control of both banks of the Straits was essential to this strategy, and more satisfactorily addresses the realistic demands of a mighty kingdom such as the Trojan one than does the isolated, inexplicably powerful city that emerges from the *Iliad*. In keeping with this train of thought, Troy was actually the ancient name of the country of the Trojans, while Ilion was the name of its capital city.

For the sake of argument, we can posit that the Trojans were roughly equally divided between the European and Asian sides, with smaller numbers occupying islands like Lemnos.

Meanwhile, after a long period of chaos and Trojan aggression, the Greeks had recovered sufficiently to begin to expand their range, deploying the greatest seafaring capability of all the regional peoples. But they were divided into warring clans. Eventually, the Greeks must have become fed up with the depredations and/or exactions of the Trojans on their shipping through the Straits; and they presumably bore a deep grudge against them for the devastating attacks that the Trojans had conducted against them over the years.

So roughly around 900 BC the Greeks overcame their incessant quarrels in a bid to smash the Trojan monopoly of the Straits and get their hands on the rich booty the city of Ilion offered. The Greeks were able to put many tens of thousands of men on the field for years on end. This gave them a significant numerical superiority over the Trojans on the Anatolian side, because the Greek fleet could blockade the Straits area and thereby split the Trojan forces in three, preventing the European and island contingents from coming to Ilion's aid. Also, naval superiority permitted the Greeks immediately to open the Black Sea to shipping and thereby to obtain supplies and trading advantage to ease the financial burden of the long war.

Once Ilion fell, the "European" Trojans had three options: fight—probably to the death against superior numbers of Greeks; permit themselves to be subjugated or enslaved by the triumphant Greeks; or escape. Their merchants and adventurers must have been familiar with

Balkan trade routes, so it was natural that they would escape through present-day Bulgaria and the former Yugoslavia. Settling in the Balkans was not an attractive option: too close to Greece for comfort. So the Trojans had a choice between heading north into Central Europe or turning west into northern Italy, and they chose the latter.

The close linguistic resemblance of "Trojan" (Troyan) and "Dorian" suggests that the Dorian invasion of the Peloponnesus and Aegean involved "trojanized" Greeks—parallel to the phenomenon of "etruscanized" Romans discussed below—which in turn might explain the extreme militarism of the Dorian Spartans and their domination of the helots. The silence of Greek sources about the history of the Dark Age between 1200 and 900 BC and the lack of more than heroic myths may constitute a tacit cover-up of the embarrassing reality that the Dark Age of Greece had been an age of Trojan ascendancy.

Becoming Etruscan

The Trojans' military prowess and relatively advanced technology permitted them to dominate the less organized local Italian peoples. In turn, the locals did not have a clue who these "Etruscans" were (although many observers have noted the linguistic similarity of the words "Trojan" and "Etruscan"). At least some Greeks, however, knew very well that they were escaped Trojans. The Trojans on Lemnos and other islands, encircled by the Greek fleet, eventually succumbed to Greek conquest, colonization, and assimilation, as did any surviving Anatolian Trojans.

In other words, two highly plausible assumptions—that the Trojans were roughly equally present on the two shores of the Straits and that the Greeks wielded naval superiority—explain how the Greeks won the war (by dividing the Trojan forces). They also account for why the Trojans could have been so severely defeated, yet show up not long after in sufficient numbers to conquer much of northern and central Italy, and why the only language traditionally connected with Etruscan is Lemniac (the Rhaetian of the Alps was spoken by Etruscans who had escaped the Celtic invasion of northern Italy in the fourth century BC).

In Italy, the Trojans/Etruscans swiftly conquered the main towns of Etruria, then apparently herded the rural population at swordpoint into these urban centers. Very roughly around 800 BC, they seem to have conquered Latium, including Rome. The exceptional skill and ferocity of relatively small contingents of Etruscans allowed them to dominate much greater numbers of Italic peoples in cities like Perugia and Rome. Many historians have recognized that Roman accounts of the early years of Rome deserve little credence and seriously underplay the role of the Etruscans.

The Etruscan role went deeper than merely providing cultural artifacts that the Romans borrowed. How exactly the Etruscans related to their more numerous *Latinii* underlings remains shrouded in obscurity; but a logical explanation would be that the hundreds or thousands of Etruscan warriors who enforced the kings' rule gradually intermarried with *Latinii*, and these Etruscan-*Latinii* spoke among themselves a parlance that grafted an Italic, Indo-European vocabulary onto an Etruscan grammar[114] (using that grammar had great snob appeal), forming the basis of the classical Latin of the patrician class. One can hypothesize that the patricians also pronounced Latin in an Etruscan manner, for instance, in the pronunciation of c's as k's and v's as w's: *Veni, vidi, vici* pronounced *Weni, widi, wiki*.

These patricians—the quisling class of Etruscan Rome—also retained the Etruscan (Trojan) military and cultural ethos, though the leaders of the Romans who subsequently overthrew the Etruscan king Tarquin the Proud were not eager to remind people that they themselves had descended, at least in part, from the Etruscan elite and had been its lackeys.[115] As the Dorians were trojanized Greeks, so were the patricians etruscanized *Latinii*.

Thus the fundamental, distinctive characteristics of Rome that led to its disciplined, aggressive, enormously successful military expansion and its

---

[114] The Turkic-speaking soldiers who were the original speakers of Hindi and Urdu left a roughly parallel grammatical imprint.

[115] Thus there were two great embarrassments that needed to be hidden by a melange of myths: that the Trojans on the European shore of the straits had run away from the Greeks, and that the Romans had been dominated for centuries by the Etruscans.

well-organized civic life were neither home-grown nor borrowed from the Etruscans, but rather were part-and-parcel of the Trojan-Etruscan inheritance of the Roman people, and specifically of the close-knit, patrician class.

Ugric Latin

In this context, the befuddlement of poor Indo-Europeans—whether the Roman plebs or modern students—over classical Latin makes profound sense. Latin has a grammar that clearly places it within the large Ural-Altaic family. In fact, we can be more specific. For a long time various Hungarian scholars have argued that Etruscan was related to Hungarian (Magyar). A book by Italian linguist Mario Alinei refines and buttresses this argument.[116] Alinei finds a remarkable resemblance between Etruscan and ancient Magyar magistrature names as well as similarities in typologies, vocabulary, and historical grammar between Etruscan and Hungarian. Like some Hungarian scholars, he posits a "theory of continuity" that places Hungarians as inhabiting the Carpathian-Danubian area from a much earlier time than other evidence suggests.

But the argument here is that in fact the Trojans/Etruscans were Ugric-speaking cousins of the Hungarians, not Hungarians themselves. The Hungarians continued to live in the steppes north of the Black Sea during the long centuries of the histories of the Trojans, Etruscans, and Romans. The Ugric branch of the Finno-Ugric language group (itself a subset of the Ural-Altaic language family) thus included four languages: the languages of the Khanty and Mantsi peoples of Siberia, Magyar, and Trojan/Etruscan. In terms of grammar, the Ugric branch included a fifth language as well: Latin.

This account of the origin of Latin lends the study of Latin greater value than it would otherwise possess, for a student actually learns the basic

---

[116] Mario Alinei, *Etrusco. Una forma arcaica di ungherese* (Bologna: Le edizioni del Mulino, 2003). For a revealing side-by-side comparison of Latin and Magyar, see http://member.melbpc.org.au/~tmajlath/magyarlatin.html.

grammar of one major group of languages and the vocabulary of another one. It also explains why the phenomenon of vowel harmony, highly characteristic of Ural-Altaic languages, is very rare in French and Spanish, yet can be found in early Latin (e.g., "*proxumus*" instead of "*proximus*", Terence, *Andria* 636) and is common in Italian dialects (from Etruscan influence) and in Romanian (from Magyar influence).

And the pattern went deeper than linguistics. Via this cultural transmission belt, a specific disciplined, aggressive steppe pattern of ordering human society formed the template for much of what came later in the history of Western Civilization. Obviously, the Roman way of doing things remained but one of competing traditions—yet an especially prevalent and recurringly dominant one.

The Phaistos Disk Seems to Be Trojan

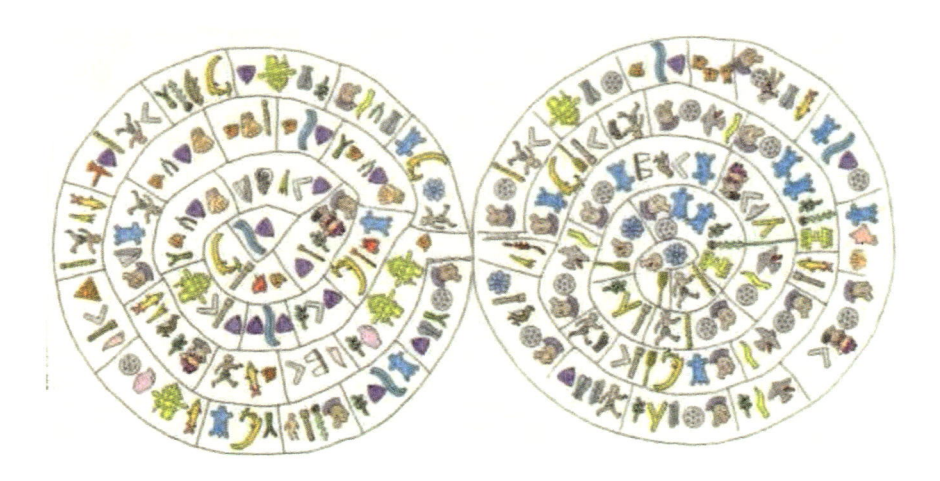

Figure 27. The Phaistos Disk

The Trojan Origin of Roman Civilization (TORC) comes with a corollary.

The famous spiral disk (here in color to aid analysis) found in Phaistos, Crete in 1908 has long defied efforts to translate it, or even to identify the language in which it is written or what kind of a document it might be.

Though many scholars and amateurs have proposed theories and even translations, none has seemed persuasive to the great majority of observers. A skeptical view holds that the disk is a forgery, but most scholars reject this. Many scholars agree that the small sample of language in the disk makes a breakthrough very unlikely unless and until other samples of the writing are found.

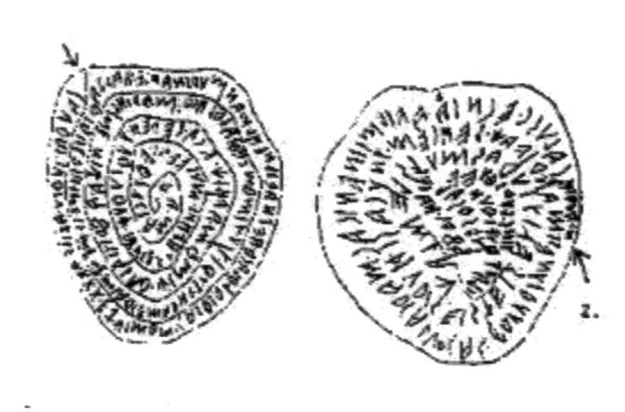

Figure 28. The Magliano Disk

The 5th Century BC Etruscan Magliano disk resembles the Phaistos disk. But the Phaistos disk is generally dated no later than 1000 BC, and often much earlier.

The Trojan Origin of Roman Civilization (TORC) can help make sense of the Phaistos disk. Even if this theory doesn't lead to a translation, it could tell us what language the disk is written in and what kind of a document it is. Knowing those two attributes of the disk might prove at least as useful for the study of ancient history as being able to read the entire text itself.

In keeping with Trojan dominance in the period around 1200 BC and for at least two centuries thereafter, according to TORC, raiding parties of Trojans had previously been among the Sea Peoples of Egyptian history and the Philistines. It would therefore make sense that they had also attacked Crete, leaving the Phaistos Disk behind.

So we can offer what must be recognized as a provisional proof that the Phaistos disk was Trojan:

First, if the Etruscans were indeed Trojans, then the fact that the Magliano disk is the only object resembling the Phaistos disk clearly suggests that they came from the same cultural tradition, though perhaps some 700 years apart—i.e., that the Phaistos disk is Trojan.

Second, aside from the general shape and spiral pattern of the two disks, most scholars consider that the lettering on the Phaistos disk is to be read starting at the parallel spot and in the same direction as the writing on the Magliano disk. To the extent that these arguments are independent of the Magliano disk, they constitute a logical pattern that connects the two disks aside from their obvious resemblance.

Third, many scholars consider that the Phaistos disk is written in a syllabary. According to TORC, the Trojan language had an Ugric grammar, and therefore belonged to the Ural-Altaic family. Ural-Altaic languages are well suited to the use of syllabaries, as can be seen in Japanese Katakana script.

Fourth, the words at the end of the Phaistos disk seem to be shorter than those at the outset, which would match the pattern found in various Ural-Altaic languages where the terminal words are frequently verbs of being or doing following longer participial and gerundive constructions.

Fifth, the frequent "warrior" plus "shield" characters at the beginning of words in the Phaistos disk could be a kind of religious incantation—perhaps an honorific name of individual gods, as with saints in Christian religious documents. The Magliano disk, which has been partially translated, is known to include the names of various Etruscan gods. So a sign of incantation or honorific names would tend to lead us to believe that the Phaistos disk contains a religious text.

Sixth, some researchers have argued that the disk's characters are derived from Luwian hieroglyphs, yet they are not sufficiently close to Luwian to permit a reading. This would be consistent with a situation in which the Trojans borrowed the concept of writing with such characters as well as some of the characters themselves from the neighboring Luwians.

Numbers 2-6 in this "proof" are mere straws in the wind. But Number 1 is not. It strongly suggests that the Phaistos disk is a Trojan religious document—if credence is given to the TORC theory. Therefore, it seems advisable to term these six points a provisional proof, and to search for further patterns in the two disks, in Etruscan religious writings, and in Etruscan vocabulary and grammar that could lead to a more definitive proof.

Chapter 12

Strategic Mistakes of World Wars I and II

In this chapter we take a giant step from ancient into modern history, and we also step into a different kind of theoretical history. Instead of using theory to examine evidence, detect underlying patterns, and explain what really happened, we engage in theorizing about what *could* have happened. "What if?" history of this sort can help us understand better what actually happened, and it can provide cautionary lessons for the future. Here we limit ourselves to examining the record of Germany in World Wars I and II and of Japan in World War II. Why just the losers' mistakes? Because they were more fateful and thus remind us that strategies and decisions can matter more in warfare than numbers of combatants or industrial might.

Key German Mistakes in World War I

In World War I Imperial Germany faced the daunting task of fighting Great Britain, France, and Russia at the same time. Mindful of the unfairness inherent in passing judgment in hindsight, we can nonetheless usefully ask whether Germany might have won the war, even against these odds, had it not made too many serious mistakes. Here is a list of key German mistakes, omitting errors at the battlefield level, in this colossal human tragedy.

1. Long before the war broke out, Germany invested great resources in a surface fleet, always a long-shot to match Britain's Royal Navy, even as German efforts to do so threatened and antagonized the British, driving them into the arms of France and Russia. Germany's surface fleet made virtually no contribution to its war effort.
2. Germany invested in colonies that proved vulnerable to British, French, and Japanese seizure in wartime.
3. In July 1914 Germany gave Austria-Hungary a blank check to crush Serbia even though the not-hard-to-predict outcome would be a two-front war against Russia, France, and the UK.
4. Germany revised its Schlieffen Plan to invade France through the Netherlands and Belgium to exclude the Netherlands, thereby perhaps lowering the chances of success, as well as missing out on the value of harnessing the economic resources of a conquered Netherlands. In other ways, Germany also whittled down the Schlieffen Plan, though whether it might have succeeded if 70,000 troops had not been shifted to confront the Russian invasion of East Prussia remains a hard-to-judge point. In general, one can argue that the Germans should have stuck to the original Schlieffen Plan or else tried something very different.
5. Germany underestimated the speed with which the British and Russians could mobilize and transport to the field.
6. Germany did not develop a Plan B in the (likely) event that the risky Schlieffen Plan would fail. This would have entailed planning for a long war and developing a resource base and stockpiles for it. This failure in planning led to terrible hunger and debilitation of the German people as well as to degradation of the civilian economy and the war effort.
7. Germany managed its wartime economy with military-like regulations instead of by using incentives that could have gained more popular support and stimulated higher productivity.

8. Germany used an attritional strategy on the Western Front even though its enemies had greater manpower and resources.
9. Germany failed to try to conquer Italy to gain industrial and agricultural resources as well as to knock a vulnerable enemy out of the war.
10. Germany failed to perceive that Russia was so weakened and its government so discredited by January 1917 that it would not be able to sustain a war effort. So Germany could have waited until a Russian collapse, then fought on to victory or a stalemate/truce against Britain and France instead of declaring unrestricted submarine warfare, which was highly likely to bring the United States into the war. But Germany rushed ahead and declared unrestricted submarine warfare anyway. Counter to wishful German thinking, this did not bring the British to their knees, even as it led the United States to enter the war. In the process, the Germans also underestimated the ability of the Americans rapidly to mobilize and put troops into combat on the Western Front. The naval command's assurance that U-boats would sink the American troop ships proved to be one more unrealistic supposition.
11. Germany underestimated Allied intelligence capabilities, leading, for instance, to the interception and deciphering of the Zimmermann Telegram, which inflamed American public opinion and made a declaration of war even more likely.

The mistakes of Germany's allies Austria-Hungary, Ottoman Turkey, and Bulgaria contributed to the disastrous outcome. In a more general sense, Germany's over-reliance on its military leaders and the incompetent Kaiser Wilhelm II lay behind many of its mistakes, while unrealistically optimistic and even reckless decision-making led to others. Thus we must conclude that Germany was not at all fated to lose the Great War, even against such fearful odds. Its leaders' shortsighted and at times downright foolish decisions played a major role in its defeat. Of course, Germany's enemies made their share of mistakes as well.

Key German Mistakes in World War II

Figure 29. Hitler and His Generals

By all accounts, Nazi Germany made serious errors in waging World War II that kept it from achieving much greater success, though whether it could have won the War remains open to doubt, given the American effort to develop nuclear weapons. Also, Japanese mistakes must be taken into consideration.

Here is a list of key German mistakes that can guide our thinking about the many lessons we can learn from this greatest of wars (not included are significant errors at the battlefield level such as at Dunkirk and Stalingrad). Of course, this list assumes that Germany's decision to go to war in the first place, with the goals it had for doing so, made sense. I thank my students for their contributions to the list.

Economic

1. Did not completely mobilize its war economy soon enough.
2. Did not draft women into the economy until the 1940s.
3. Starved and shot Soviet POWs instead of using them as slave labor.
4. Wasted resources to destroy the Jews, who could have boosted the economy in ordinary jobs or as slave laborers.
5. Diverted supplies from the *Wehrmacht* to the SS and other units.

Political

1. Permitted endless bureaucratic infighting and duplication.
2. Alienated the populations of occupied territories, especially in the USSR, where many initially opposed Stalin.

Military

1. Chose to fight the Battle of Britain against high odds (a stack of contingencies: the RAF, the Royal Navy, securing a beachhead, the British army, U.S. support), yet failed to concentrate on the greatest British vulnerabilities: fighter plane production, the electrical grid, and sea lanes that could have been cut by bombers from France and Norway.
2. Did not coordinate with Japan against the USSR.
3. Allowed Mussolini to foul things up instead of clamping down on or removing him.
4. Chose to attack the USSR instead of first driving the British out of the Mediterranean and Middle East, thus opting to fight a two-front war.
5. Delayed the German attack on the USSR to handle the Balkans sideshow, yet didn't prepare for winter.
6. Put too much emphasis on north and south in the 1941 attack on the USSR, and delayed the crucial fall offensive against Moscow to focus on Kiev.
7. Did not attack Moscow and the main Soviet forces in Spring 1942.
8. Underestimated Soviet resilience, defense production, and military prowess.
9. Underestimated American industrial, technological, and fighting capabilities.
10. Declared war on the U.S., sparing it the dilemma over Europe First vs Pacific War.
11. Failed to comprehend and counteract the Allies' great superiority in intelligence and deception.

Key Japanese Mistakes in World War II

When Japan went to war against the United States in 1941, its chances of winning were slim, indeed. But it is worth asking what steps Japan might have taken, or what mistakes it might have avoided, to increase the likelihood of greater success and possibly even victory. Without dwelling on specific battles or on mistakes such as conducting Banzai charges against machine guns and fueling planes on the decks of aircraft carriers, we can identify a series of strategic errors that led to less success and ensured more rapid defeat.

1. Before the war, Japan invested heavily in large battleships and cruisers instead of submarines and anti-submarine warfare. Other countries made the same mistake, but Japan lacked the economic resources to overcome it.
2. If we assume that conquering Manchuria made sense, Japan erred by then trying to conquer ever greater pieces of China with massive inputs of men and materiel, incurring substantial losses without achieving victory even as it antagonized the United States.
3. Japan failed to follow up immediately on its Pearl Harbor attack by conquering the Hawaiian Islands, which would have opened up the possibility to disrupt the Panama Canal and set up bases on the west coast of South America and in the South Pacific to isolate Australia and New Zealand. An essential step would have been to sink one or both U.S. aircraft carriers in the central Pacific, which was well within Japan's capabilities.
4. Japan failed to follow up on its victories at Colombo and Trincomalee to destroy the British fleet in the Indian Ocean. This would have permitted it to blockade India, reduce supplies to the Chinese Nationalists, cut off Australia and New Zealand from the west, block the Red Sea route to British Egypt, block supply to the Soviet Union via Iran, and destroy or appropriate British oil assets in the Gulf. True, the Japanese fleet was worn down after a long cruise, but it could have sent its damaged ships back to Japan while pressing on against a fleeing enemy. Such body blows against British imperial assets would have significantly aided Germany. Even though Nazi Germany was uncooperative, arrogant, and racist, Japan had no choice but to do everything possible to help it win the war because a German defeat would doom the Japanese.

5. When the Germans attacked the Soviet Union in 1941 (without alerting the Japanese), Japan could have shifted a million or more soldiers from China and elsewhere to conquer the Soviet Far East and ever larger portions of Siberia, thus dividing the Soviet war effort and shutting off war production from Siberia. Such an attack would have yielded only modest direct benefits to Japan; but it could have contributed to a German victory over the Soviets, which would have been of inestimable benefit to the Japanese.
6. Instead of using Japanese or local civilian administrators, Japan let its army administer the conquered countries. The army imposed harsh martial law and disrupted trade, alienating many potential contributors to the Japanese war effort.
7. The Japanese failed to perceive and counteract the great U.S. superiority in intelligence, leading to disasters at Midway and other battles.

With the unfair benefit of hindsight, we can see that Japan should have focused above all on finding ways to help Nazi Germany win, however unlovable and uncooperative the Germans were. Pushing the Americans back to their west coast, dominating the Indian Ocean, and conquering much of Siberia were arguably within Japan's grasp and would have significantly aided the German war effort. Still, even if German and Japanese attacks had knocked the Soviet Union out of the war, the Axis powers would have to attack the mighty United States and keep it from developing nuclear weapons, two very demanding tasks. Be that as it may, bold and insightful thinking could have made a Japanese victory much more conceivable. Of course, the realities of army-navy disputes, cultural insularity, and the fog of war made such thinking hard to do, and acting on it even harder.

Chapter 13

Carroll Quigley, Theorist of Civilizations

Before we examine some famous fatal moments of American history, let's take a look at an historian who was well known by the cognoscenti but otherwise wrongly ignored: Carroll Quigley.[117] Quigley was remarkable for his terrific energy, unusual breadth and depth of learning, and penetrating intellect. His work touched upon certain of the episodes and themes of this book, providing a model of how to work in a highly conceptual, interdisciplinary manner with the evidence of the past.

*****

Carroll Quigley (1910-1977) was a noted historian, polymath, and theorist of the evolution of civilizations.

Born and raised in Boston, Quigley planned to pursue a career in biochemistry. But he soon shifted to history, to which he brought an analytical, scientific approach and a questing

---
[117] I was a student of Quigley and knew him personally.

spirit. After receiving a B.A., M.A., and Ph.D in history from Harvard University,[118] he taught at Princeton and Harvard. In 1941 Quigley joined the School of Foreign Service at Georgetown University, where he came to teach a highly regarded course, "Development of Civilization".

Endowed with a Napoleonic constitution and willing to work 16 hours a day, Quigley was a rapid, retentive reader who devoured the contents of thousands of books and came to possess an exceptional range of knowledge in many fields. Not one to hide his light under a bushel basket, he claimed to have read everything worth reading. Fields of his special expertise included aspects of prehistoric culture (e.g., primitive poison fishhooks), the impact of weapons technology on social organization, and the Anglo-American elite.

Quigley emphasized "inclusive diversity" as a value of Western Civilization long before diversity became a commonplace, and he denounced Platonic doctrines as an especially pernicious deviation from this ideal. Quigley argued that the reintroduction of Aristotle's teachings in the Middle Ages, most notably in the work of Thomas Aquinas, led Western Civilization away from Platonism and onto the track of a highly fruitful approach to knowledge based on scientific observation and experimentation, and driven by ethical concerns.

As a spell-binding lecturer, Quigley made a strong impression on many of his students, including future U.S. President Bill Clinton, who referred to Quigley in his acceptance speech to the 1992 Democratic National Convention, saying:

> As a teenager, I heard John Kennedy's summons to citizenship. And then, as a student at Georgetown, I heard that call clarified by a professor named Carroll Quigley, who said to us that America was the greatest Nation in history because our people had always believed in two things—that tomorrow can be better than today and that every one of us has a personal moral responsibility to make it so.

---

[118] His doctoral dissertation was on the Napoleonic Kingdom of Italy.

According to Clinton's biographers, he developed a relationship with Quigley and considered him his guru. During his presidency, Clinton made no mention of Quigley in public but was said to refer to him repeatedly inside the White House. At times Clinton also used Quigley's concepts and formulations without attribution in impromptu remarks that enhanced his reputation as a thinker. When after his time in office he once listed his three favorite Georgetown teachers, however, Quigley was not one of them. Was Clinton hiding his deep indebtedness to Quigley for fear that people would (however unfairly) view him as a mere epigone of his revered mentor? Or did Clinton distance himself from Quigley because he believed derogatory rumors about his one-time guru (see below)?

In the 1950s Quigley did some consulting for the U.S. Department of Defense, the U.S. Navy, the Smithsonian Institution, and the House Select Committee on Astronautics and Space Exploration. A sought-after lecturer, Quigley also served as a book reviewer for the *Washington Star*, and was a contributor to and editorial board member of *Current History*.

Quigley authored two influential books: *The Evolution of Civilizations* (1961) and *Tragedy and Hope: A History of the World in Our Time* (1966). Two other books were published posthumously from his manuscripts: *The Anglo-American Establishment* (1981) and *Weapons Systems and Political Stability, a History* (1983). Quigley's efforts to have *Tragedy and Hope* reprinted by Macmillan were thwarted in a manner that led him to write that certain powerful interests were seeking to suppress him, or at least his book. In fact, the book sharply criticized various individuals and groups, most pointedly the U.S. Air Force and the associated military-industrial complex, so his suspicion may well have been warranted.

Although he received only limited public and professional recognition for his contributions, Quigley was in fact a leading theorist of the rise and fall of civilizations. He developed a 7-stage model (Mixture, Gestation, Expansion, Age of Conflict, Universal Empire, Decay, and Invasion) integrated into a framework of analysis that included dimensions of power (military and political), wealth (economic and social), and outlook (intellectual and religious). His illuminating discussion of the geographical and climatic matrix in which a civilization develops, his critical interpretation of the political and epistemological underpinnings of ancient philosophy, and his analysis of the mechanisms of expansion and conflict stages of civilization were a good deal more scientific and well-grounded than the more literary efforts of previous historians of civilizations.

The penetrating originality of Quigley's analytical mind, his flow of novel concepts, his penchant for provocative formulations, his ceaseless crossing of disciplinary boundaries, and his willingness to challenge specialists and authorities in at times caustic language led to a fair amount of controversy, though in fact his political and social views were moderate. Quigley was an early and fierce critic of the Vietnam War; and he inveighed against the activities of the military-industrial complex that, in his mind, were threatening to transform the United States into an empire, thereby dooming it to eventual corruption, fossilization, and decline. He was ever on the alert for signs of the processes by which a dynamic "instrument" of society that satisfied the needs of individuals could turn into a stagnant, self-aggrandizing "institution".

A central concern of Quigley was whether Western Civilization could renew its best traditions—including investing in innovation and emphasizing spiritual values and interpersonal relations rather than material things—after the Age of Conflict between 1895 and 1945, or whether it would slide into an era of Universal Empire.[119] Initially full of hope on this subject, he grew more pessimistic about it in his later

---

[119] Quigley's approach to the future of the United States emphasized the need to consider American problems in the context of Western Civilization, not just as a question of the rise and fall of great powers; and to think about change in terms of his seven stages of the evolution of civilizations. He does not seem to have developed a full set of criteria for determining when a civilization had moved from an Age of Crisis into a Universal Empire, though his lecturing and writing, e.g., about the Roman Empire, contained aspects of such criteria. Complicating matters, he had noted the remarkable capacity of Western Civilization in the past to shift from an Age of Crisis (the fourth stage) back into a new Age of Expansion (the third stage), and in the 1945-1970 era he was hopeful that this was occurring. Also, according to Quigley, appearances could deceive in a Universal Empire; it would have a superficial prosperity (a Golden Age) and internal peace, with wars only on the periphery. But beneath the surface, decay would set in, for instance, in the political and social spheres. At any rate, his writings provide components of such criteria for those seeking to develop a full set of them and apply it to the cases of the United States and of Western Civilization as a whole.

years. Quigley said of himself that he was a conservative defending the liberal tradition of the West.

Quigley became well known among those who believe that there is an international conspiracy to bring about a one-world government. In *Tragedy and Hope*, he based his analysis on his research in the papers of the Anglo-American elite that, he held, secretly sought to control the U.S. and UK governments through a series of Round Table Groups. The Round Table group in the United States was the Council on Foreign Relations, connected with the J.P. Morgan banking cluster. He argued that before 1950 the Republican and (less so) the Democratic parties were controlled by an "international Anglophile network" that shaped elections, though he also pointed out how the unrealistic thinking of some people in this network contributed to appeasement of Hitler, while in general the Round Table was less capable of influencing world developments than it aspired to be.

Even as conspiracy theorists assailed Quigley for his approval of the goals (not the tactics) of the Anglo-American elite, they selectively used his information and analysis as evidence for their views. Quigley himself thought that the influence of the Anglo-American elite had waned after World War II and that, in American society after 1965, the problem was that no elite was in charge and acting responsibly.

No matter how reasonable Quigley's thinking on this and other subjects was, the association of his findings with the kooky, paranoid fantasies of right wing conspiracy theorists, in combination with the sheer originality of his ideas and his drive to find and articulate underlying patterns, caused rumors to circulate about his mental status. His detractors, including jealous colleagues, an ambitious dean, and various enemies, were quick to criticize him and continued to denigrate him for decades after his death, while he and his contributions were, with few exceptions, ignored by historians and the media.

Toward the end of his Georgetown career, Quigley ran into criticism from students unhappy about his grading (he was an old-fashioned grader), was roughed up in class by student antiwar protesters, and gave up his "Development of Civilization" course because an academic power game had attached unacceptable conditions to it. He became more distrustful, at times deeply so. Still, he continued to espouse an optimistic vision of the potential of humankind and of the liberal values of Western Civilization. Eventually he retired to work on his book manuscripts.

Nowadays, Quigley is often spoken of in reference to his writings about the Anglo-American Establishment or as an influence on Clinton. But his theory of the evolution of civilizations, his methods of thinking, his multitudinous concepts, and his philosophy of social good have much more general and enduring importance. Among other things, they provide a valuable framework for understanding the interaction of civilizations in a global era as well as suggesting pathways to the future for Western Civilization. In addition, Quigley's teachings and his dynamic persona had a profound impact on thousands of students and intellectuals, with outcomes that we are not yet in a position fully to assess.

Chapter 14

Did the KGB Arrange the Assassination of John F. Kennedy?

Figure 31. Lee Harvey Oswald

New evidence and analysis suggest that the KGB bears a significant share of the responsibility for the 1963 assassination of President John F. Kennedy.

Official investigations have tended to discount the likelihood of a Soviet hand in the assassination, and few outside investigators have pursued this line of inquiry. However, some observers have always considered the Soviets a likely suspect. The Soviets had a palpable, powerful motive: to gain revenge for the humiliation of the USSR in the 1962 Cuban missile crisis.

Certainly, the idiosyncratic odyssey of Lee Harvey Oswald into the Soviet Union and a Russian marriage, as well as his contacts with Soviet diplomatic offices preceding the assassination, afforded the KGB many opportunities to interact with him. In a sense, therefore, the KGB is the elephant in the living room of suspects in this case. Yet repeated investigations have failed to turn up specific evidence that would implicate the KGB.

Now a new report (see below: "Did the KGB Murder Mary Meyer?") details the evidence and logic for thinking that, one year after the Kennedy assassination, the KGB used a contract killer to murder Mary Pinchot Meyer, JFK's senior female consort during his White House years. If we accept this conclusion, and there is telling circumstantial evidence of its accuracy, then we must ask what it suggests about the assassination of JFK himself.

Figure 32. John F. Kennedy and Mary Meyer

Three aspects of the Meyer case deserve consideration. Individually, they are mere straws in the wind; but cumulatively they become more interesting.

First, the KGB must have had a compelling reason to murder Mary Pinchot Meyer. Otherwise, it is hard to see why they would have taken the risk of exposure. The most plausible motive would have been to get revenge against Meyer for misleading Khrushchev and the KGB about Kennedy (she was acting as a behind-the-scenes intermediary between Kennedy and Khrushchev, with an apparent personal agenda of promoting peace via marijuana- and LSD-induced softening of American and Soviet leaders—see below).

According to Ion Mihai Pacepa, at the time deputy director of foreign intelligence for Gheorghe Gheorghiu-Dej's Romania, in his book *Programmed to Kill: Lee Harvey Oswald, the Soviet KGB, and the Kennedy Assassination*,[120] Gheorghiu-Dej was visiting Moscow at the time of the Cuban Missile Crisis. Pacepa writes:

> According to Dej's account, when Khrushchev finished reading that cable [from the KGB in Washington saying that Kennedy had ordered a naval quarantine of Cuba], his face was purple. He looked

---

[120] (Chicago: Ivan R. Dee, 2007), 185

inquiringly at [KGB chief] Semichastny, and, when the terrified general nodded, Khrushchev "cursed like a bargeman". Then he threw Semichastny's cable on the floor and ground his heel into it. "That's how I'm going to crush that viper," he cried. The "viper", Dej explained in telling the story, was Kennedy.

Goading himself on, Khrushchev grew increasingly hysterical, uttering violent threats against the 'millionaire's whore' and his CIA masters.

Dej interpreted "that viper" and the 'millionaire's whore' as references to Kennedy, but viper (*gadyuka*) is feminine in Russian and a common epithet for a malicious, treacherous woman. Moreover, Kennedy was a millionaire himself and of the wrong gender, and he did not have CIA masters. A far better interpretation is that Khrushchev was referring to Mary Meyer. In turn, this suggests that Meyer's peace rhetoric and her talk about the purported use of drugs by American leaders had emboldened Khrushchev to undertake his breathtakingly reckless Cuban missile adventure, which ultimately led to a deeply embarrassing withdrawal. However, the close fit with Meyer did not mean that Khrushchev was not after Kennedy; rather, it showed that he was eager for vengeance, and that would clearly include Kennedy as well.

Second, the timing of both killings was right. Meyer was not murdered several years before or after the JFK assassination, but 11 months after— enough time for it not to seem too closely connected, but not any more time than that. So, too, Kennedy was murdered 13 months after the Cuban missile crisis, not a year sooner or later, though that seems to have been a result of the semi-freelance action of Lee Harvey Oswald in seizing the opportunity of Kennedy's visit to Dallas.

Third, the divorced husband of Meyer was senior CIA official Cord Meyer. When questioned by a reporter as he neared death in 2001, he said that his ex-wife was murdered by "[t]he same sons of bitches that killed John F. Kennedy."[121] This statement has been taken to refer to the CIA,

---

[121] C. David Heymann, *The Georgetown Ladies' Social Club* (New York: Atria Books, 2003), 168. In his 1980/82 book *Facing Reality: From World Federalism to the CIA* (Washington, D.C.: University Press of America, 1982), Cord Meyer denied reports that he was convinced that his ex-wife had been murdered by the

but that makes no sense. There is no good reason to think that CIA was involved in the murder of Kennedy, despite strained efforts by conspiracy theorists (and Soviet disinformation) to show otherwise. Nor is there any valid reason to think that the CIA wanted to murder Mary Pinchot Meyer, who was a long-standing friend of Agency officials. (This has not stopped some from suggesting that the CIA murdered her to cover up its assassination of Kennedy.[122])

But, if one assumes the CIA knew that the KGB had murdered Mary Pinchot Meyer, then Cord Meyer's remark takes on a very different meaning. It is a statement by a former senior CIA official that he, and presumably the Agency in general, had concluded that the KGB was behind the murder of John F. Kennedy.

The KGB's Favorite U.S. Marine

The Soviets repeatedly denied that the KGB had had any contact with Lee Harvey Oswald, and at first they seem to have been suspicious of him. But as a Marine radar specialist in Japan and California, Oswald had access to extensive classified information regarding radars, flight patterns, and in particular the new US height-finding radar that would have been of exceptional interest to the KGB in regard to the U-2 spy flights. Oswald told US Embassy officials in Moscow that he intended to reveal sensitive information to the Soviets. Gary Powers, pilot of the U-2 flight downed in May, 1960, suggested that Oswald might have betrayed to the Soviets information that they used to shoot down the U-2.[123] This seems very believable, and it would mean that Oswald had proved himself a loyal

---

Soviets. He wrote that he trusted the D.C. police's conclusion that the crime had been a sex or robbery case (p. 144). But this would not apply to Kennedy's assassination, so his denial is not to be believed, especially since he later contradicted it.

[122] Peter Janney, *Mary's Mosaic. The CIA Conspiracy to Murder John F. Kennedy, Mary Pinchot Meyer, and Their Vision for World Peace* (New York: Skyhorse Publishing, 2012)

[123] Francis Gary Powers and Curt Gentry, *Operation Overflight: A Memoir of the U-2 Incident* (New York: Holt, Rinehart and Winston, 1970), 357-9

communist and one who had provided precious information to the USSR. So the KGB would have trusted him.

Given Oswald's aggressive mentality and track record (well known to the KGB), it would have required very little for the KGB to insert into his mind the suggestion that he should assassinate Kennedy. Indeed, virulent communist hate propaganda during Oswald's years in the Soviet Union might have instilled in his impressionable brain the need to take action, as the occasion presented itself, against those like the American president who thwarted the progress of communism.

According to Pacepa, there are reasons to think that, under cover of a civilian life in Minsk, Oswald was trained by the KGB in clandestine techniques for serving as an operative if and when he returned to the United States. As Pacepa persuasively shows, the KGB provided Oswald his wife Marina according to a standard technique to bind a foreign agent to the USSR.

Otherwise reliable defector Yurii Nosenko's denial of KGB interest in Oswald, Pacepa points out, was wrong because Nosenko was in the domestic division of the KGB and was not aware of the interest of the KGB's foreign branch (PGU) in him. Thus Pacepa's explanation trumps standard "Lone Gunman" accounts by capable authors who have convincingly debunked a host of conspiracy theories but have themselves mistakenly followed Nosenko.[124] Pacepa also argues that, even though the Soviets originally may have intended to assassinate Kennedy, in 1962 the

---

[124] Pacepa argues that he was trained as an operative based on standard KGB procedure, Pacepa, 290. When Oswald was asked about having a rifle in the USSR, he gave an evasive answer: "'Ever own a rifle in Russia?' [interrogator] Fritz asks. 'You know you can't own a rifle in Russia,' Oswald smirks.... 'I had a shotgun over there. You can't own a rifle in Russia.'" I.e., while stating the rule against ownership twice, he never addresses the evident intent of the question, to determine whether he had access to a rifle and training with it. Clearly, such access and training would have been powerfully suggestive of assassination, without a word being spoken. Thus we need not go so far as Pacepa does in arguing that the KGB, which was well aware that Oswald was a loose cannon on the deck, trained him as an operative. The suggestiveness of rifle practice would have sufficed while maintaining KGB deniability. 4 H214 Warren Commission Testimony John Will Fritz, in Vincent Bugliosi, *Four Days in November: The Assassination of President John F. Kennedy* (New York, W.W. Norton, 2007), 199

KGB ordered its agents worldwide to cease assassination activities because Khrushchev's reputation had been badly tarnished as an orderer of assassinations in a West German criminal case. Failing to receive a go-ahead from the KGB, Oswald purchased a rifle on his own, against KGB practice, and pursued his own plan to assassinate Kennedy. The KGB was alarmed enough to move Oswald's handler (George de Mohrenschildt) out of Dallas in spring 1963 and into sequestration in Haiti. But the Soviets evidently decided not to stop Oswald or warn the Americans.

Therefore, following the incisive account of General Pacepa, the most senior Soviet Bloc intelligence officer to defect during the Cold War, the answer to the question of whether the Soviets ordered the assassination of Kennedy appears to be No. But they provided the ugly, suggestive propaganda that led Oswald to hate Kennedy; conceivably but not very probably, they may have trained him as an operative, while very likely at a minimum they provided him with rifle practice; they failed to order him to desist; and they deliberately did not warn the Americans of a possible upcoming assassination attempt. Likely using the Cuban intelligence organization as a go-between, they also arranged for Jack Ruby's murder of Oswald two days after the Kennedy assassination, Pacepa argues; and (Pacepa also suggests) they killed Ruby himself with radioactive poison at the time when he was scheduled for retrial and might have become available to talk with reporters.

The contract murder of Mary Meyer would make a third KGB-arranged killing that fit into the pattern of doing away with problematical individuals connected with Kennedy and his assassination.[125]

Thus, even though Oswald ultimately acted on his own, Khrushchev and the KGB were deeply involved in the assassination of John F. Kennedy and must share the blame for it.

We now have a full, very believable explanation of the JFK assassination that contains both the idiosyncrasies of a Lone Gunman and

---

[125] The KGB must be considered the most likely perpetrator of the suspicious death of columnist Dorothy Kilgallen in 1965. The only reporter to have interviewed Jack Ruby, Kilgallen had said that she was going to reveal new information on the Kennedy assassination. True to character, Ruby appears to have misled her into thinking that the Mob had put him up to killing Oswald.

the conspiratorial maneuvering of a KGB engaged in its specialty of deniable murder. The Kennedy assassination and related murders can now be seen as an integral episode of a Cold War that America waged against a ruthless enemy. And Americans can finally feel a sense of closure about this national tragedy.

The John F. Kennedy assassination shares important traits with the anthrax mailings case of 2001 (Chapter 16). In both cases observers assigned far too much weight to objections to elephants-in-the-living-room (the KGB and al Qaeda, respectively) and not enough weight to correctly evaluated circumstantial evidence.

Meanwhile, to supplement the JFK assassination story, we can take a look at a possible KGB hand in the slaying of Mary Meyer.

Did the KGB Murder Mary Meyer?

On October 12, 1964, Mary Pinchot Meyer was murdered on the canal towpath in Georgetown.[126] A divorced artist from a prominent family, Meyer was known by insiders to have been President John F. Kennedy's senior female consort during his White House years, though the story never leaked to the public.

Her murder and the ensuing trial of Raymond Crump, Jr., an African-American laborer found by the police in the vicinity of the murder, drew a good deal of attention at the time. Crump had been identified by a gas station attendant helping start a car on a road overlooking the canal. Hearing cries of "Somebody help me. Somebody help me" and two shots, the attendant ran to look. He subsequently claimed to have seen a man dressed like Crump standing over the body a few seconds after the shots, and he said that the man put something dark into his pocket.

An Air Force lieutenant who had been jogging on the towpath reported that he had passed a woman resembling Meyer walking westward as he

---

[126] The fullest account is in Nina Burleigh, *A Very Private Woman: The Life and Unsolved Murder of Presidential Mistress Mary Meyer,* (New York: Bantam, 1998). See also Peter Janney's book, op. cit., which contains many interesting details even though it relies at times on dubious sources.

headed back eastward, and then a man roughly resembling Crump 200 yards behind her.

A policeman encountered Crump not far from the crime scene after police, alerted by the gas station attendant, had blocked the exits to the wooded area between the canal and the Potomac River. Crump was wet and jacketless on a chilly day, and his fly was open. He told the police that he had fallen asleep and his fishing rod had slipped into the water (it was later found at home). A jacket that fit Crump and that his wife said was his was found in the vicinity. A meticulous hunt including frogmen found no weapon. Crump was arrested on the basis of the evidence available.

The gunshot wounds that killed Meyer were in the back of the head and in the heart. Both wounds showed signs of being inflicted by shots fired very close to the skin.

In spite of suggestive circumstantial evidence against Crump, a D.C. jury found him not guilty. The prosecution had missed bringing some key evidence to the attention of the jury. Another exonerating factor was Crump's lawyer's presentation of him as a poor, confused, harmless little man who was being blamed for a crime he hadn't committed. The real murderer had escaped before the police closed off the exits from the area. The lawyer later told a journalist that Crump had been very uncommunicative and that he had cried when she visited him in prison. Three members of his mother's church testified that he was an upstanding young man.

Crump subsequently led a life of crime, with 22 arrests in the Washington, D.C. area, including cases of assault with a deadly weapon, arson, and rape. It is quite possible that he committed other crimes of which he was not suspected.

Mary Pinchot Meyer had previously been married to senior CIA official Cord Meyer. The day following the murder, CIA counterspy chief James Angleton was found inside her Georgetown house hunting for her diary, thought to have included sensitive information about Kennedy. When the diary was finally found some time later, it was given to Angleton. It was subsequently said to have been destroyed by CIA.

Various researchers and observers have examined the case. Their opinions are divided. Some have tried to tie Meyer's murder to the assassination of Kennedy the previous year, and a few even suggest that the CIA was involved in both. However, there is another explanation.

A Theory of the Case

When I was serving in the Department of State in the 1980s, a CIA officer told me that the KGB had murdered Kennedy's girlfriend. The KGB made the murder look like a sexual attack that went awry.

CIA found out within an hour or two, perhaps from SIGINT or perhaps from HUMINT, that in fact it was a KGB job. But CIA was evidently reluctant to reveal what it knew, so the case has gone officially unsolved for decades.

The simplest, most telling explanation would be that, in her desire to promote peace, Meyer had inadvertently misled Khrushchev into thinking that Kennedy was too weak and peace-loving to respond to Soviet missiles in Cuba. When this proved wrong and Khrushchev was humiliated, he decided to eliminate her. Thus the "viper" anecdote. A KGB contact in a D.C. neighborhood hired Crump to murder Meyer in a way that looked like a sexual assault that went awry. Crump was instructed to act dumb and even like a plausible sexual attacker, yet he could remain confident that no D.C. jury would find him guilty as long as he safely disposed of the murder gun. Crump would presumably never know that it was the KGB that was paying for his work as a contract killer.

The theory that the KGB hired Crump to murder Meyer makes sense of the available evidence regarding the case. Crump was a violent, ruthless man. His lingering in the vicinity of the crime strongly suggests that he wanted to be arrested. His weeping and other behavior were nothing more than acting. He was a contract killer who, according to this theory, unwittingly did the bidding of the KGB.

But before we accept this story, we need to take a closer look at Mary Meyer and the Cuban Missile Crisis.

Did Mary Meyer Unintentionally Set Off the Cuban Missile Crisis?

Sometimes a storyteller misses the real meaning of the story.

By all accounts, the Cuban Missile Crisis was the most dangerous episode of the Cold War. The United States and the Soviet Union came frighteningly close to launching nuclear attacks against each other. Only fear, luck, and occasionally inspired negotiating moved them onto the path of resolving the crisis—via a humiliating Soviet withdrawal in the face of U.S. nuclear superiority.

Historians have identified many motives for the initial Soviet decision to place missiles in Cuba. The Soviets wanted to rectify the imbalance of nuclear forces that favored the United States. More viscerally, as Khrushchev later noted, "The Americans had surrounded our country with military bases and threatened us with nuclear weapons, and now they would learn just what it feels like to have enemy missiles pointed at you...."[127] Deterring an American attack on Cuba, which aggressive U.S. maneuvers had made seem to be in the works, was a major goal, as were locking Cuba into the Soviet Bloc and giving an example to the rest of Latin America. Gaining leverage over Berlin and asserting leadership of worldwide communism by heading off potential Chinese support of Castro may have also played their roles.

Still, contemporary observers and later historians agree that Khrushchev took a breathtakingly reckless risk—one he ultimately had to back down from. As a September 19, 1962 CIA assessment of the Soviet buildup in Cuba put it, deploying ballistic missiles or building a submarine base "would indicate a far greater willingness to increase the level of risk in US-Soviet relations than the USSR has displayed thus far."[128] Kennedy himself said that it was "one hell of a gamble", and he ascribed it to Khrushchev's perception from the 1961 Vienna summit that he was weak.

What drove Khrushchev to take this extraordinary risk? In effect, to ask this is to ask why there was a Cuban Missile Crisis in the first place.

---

[127] Nikita Sergeevich Khrushchev, *Khrushchev Remembers* (London: Andre Deutsch, 1971), 494

[128] Robert Dallek, *An Unfinished Life. John F. Kennedy, 1917-1963* (New York: Little, Brown, 2003), 541

Kennedy's Senior Girlfriend

Though the story was kept out of the national news, Jack Kennedy was a notorious womanizer. For years he had worked his way through a succession of lovers, and neither marrying Jackie nor entering the White House cured his compulsive skirt-chasing. However, there is no evidence that any of these women had any special influence over him. Except one.

Mary Pinchot Meyer was an upper-class Pennsylvanian (her father was an isolationist with a pacifist bent) who had married Cord Meyer, a leading peace advocate who then became a CIA manager. After divorcing him in 1958, Mary began working as an abstract artist and moved in fashionable social circles. Acquainted with Kennedy since college days, she became a frequent visitor at the White House and eventually Kennedy's senior girlfriend, attending many receptions and private dinners as well as showing up for one-on-one evening sessions with the President. Unlike Kennedy's other girlfriends, though, Mary Meyer was permitted to stay for serious discussions and to attend policy meetings.[129]

Around this time, Meyer began to meet with Dr. Timothy Leary of Harvard University, famous for his experimenting with psychedelic drugs. She came to him, Leary later wrote, seeking advice on how to run LSD sessions with women in influential circles of Washington, D.C., with the goal of getting their power-elite husbands to turn on, lose their aggressive edge, and seek peace. In a later meeting, she complained to him that one of the wives had snitched on her, and that she was in trouble. Her goal, she told Leary, was to follow the prescription of poet Allen Ginsberg for achieving peace in the nuclear age. Kennedy and

---

[129] Burleigh, 194. The characterization of Mary's role is from White House Counsel Myer Feldman. Janney's book *Mary's Mosaic* reaches an untenable conclusion that includes his own CIA father, Wistar Janney, as an accessory in Mary Meyer's murder. In all likelihood, Wistar Janney learned of the murder within an hour or so of its occurrence not because there was a CIA conspiracy but because CIA had found out from SIGINT or HUMINT what the KGB had done.

Khrushchev, Ginsberg had said on various public occasions, should smoke pot together. Then the threat of war would go away.[130]

It seems likely that Meyer herself smoked marijuana and had taken her share of LSD. It must be understood that at this early date the negative impacts of LSD were not well understood, and it was not outlawed. She claimed that she had smoked pot with President Kennedy, but we have only her word for this story.[131]

How exactly Meyer carried out her peace campaign is not completely clear. We know that Kennedy was concerned that he could not communicate well with Khrushchev by relying solely on the cold warriors who populated established diplomatic and intelligence channels. Thus Mary Meyer's advocacy of peace seems to have appealed to Kennedy and could explain why he appeared to hold her in great esteem, though he also confided to Ben Bradlee that "Mary would be rough to live with."[132] He seems to have meant that she could be very demanding.

By dint of her status as the senior presidential lady friend, Mary appears to have inserted herself into the U.S.-Soviet relationship as a key go-between. It appears that she used this position to push her recipe of peace and drugs on the Soviets as well as on Kennedy. She may also have been keeping CIA informed. At any rate, she seems to have proven very persuasive with both sides, perhaps because she exaggerated how ready each was to cooperate. We do not know what she told the Soviets. That Kennedy was smoking pot with her? That other powerful men in Washington were turning on? That Kennedy was eager to resolve superpower disputes peacefully (which of course was true)? Whatever it was, it seems to have persuaded Khrushchev, who already suspected Kennedy of weakness from their encounter at the Vienna summit that Kennedy was a pushover who would acquiesce in the emplacement of Soviet missiles in Cuba.

Why should we think that this reconstruction of such behind-the-scenes interactions is accurate? Because of Pacepa's account above of Gheorghe-

---

[130] Janney, 216-7
[131] Ibid., 70
[132] Burleigh, 208

Dej's story about Khrushchev's rage over Kennedy's ordering of a naval quarantine of Cuba.

This hearsay story could have been inflated or distorted in the telling and retelling. Nonetheless, it deserves credence for four reasons. First, it has the ring of truth, being characteristic of Khrushchev's behavior. Second, Gheorghiu-Dej told and Pacepa retold the story without realizing its real meaning, and the mistaken details and explanation make its real meaning more believable because Gheorghiu-Dej and Pacepa did not intend to give it the meaning it clearly has. Third, it fits perfectly with the need for a persuasive explanation of why Khrushchev took such a risk as to put missiles into Cuba. Fourth, in fact the KGB arranged for a contract murderer to kill Mary Meyer on the Canal towpath in Georgetown in October, 1964.

Conclusions

Three conclusions suggest themselves.

First, Kennedy must share in the blame for the emergence of the Cuban Missile Crisis. His irresponsible womanizing led him into an emotional attachment where he mixed business and pleasure in such a way as to blind himself. Meyer was a pot-smoking, LSD-tripping abstract artist; a woman-about-town with a woolly scheme suggested by Allen Ginsberg; and a pushy pacifist and amateur negotiator with a supercharged sense of mission dealing with the most sensitive, consequential relationship in the world. This was an explosive combination that should have set off alarm bells in Kennedy's generally level head. But it didn't.

Second, the KGB should have seen through Meyer and warned Khrushchev, who clearly did not understand Kennedy or the United States. Khrushchev was foolish and indeed reckless to take such a gamble based on Meyer's stories.

Third, it is perhaps comforting to think that the unusual mixture of personal idiosyncrasies (of Kennedy, Khrushchev, and Meyer) and circumstances that led to such a dangerous misunderstanding occurred only once during the decades of the Cold War. But this story reminds us that the new horrors of nuclear weapons exist in close proximity to the age-old human capacity for folly.

Chapter 15

Prying the Lids off the 2001 Cover-ups

The apparent misdeeds and cover-ups of the George W. Bush administration related to the terrorist attacks of 2001 remain in historical limbo. Neither presidents, nor the Congress, nor the media have gotten to the bottom of these tragic events. The 9/11 Commission *Report*, while providing hundreds of useful details, did not ask fundamental questions and so must be considered in effect a cover-up. As a result, the American public has not come to closure on the 9/11 attacks or on the anthrax mailings of 2001, nor is there a shared understanding of the real reasons that the US attacked Iraq in 2003.

These failures have left the field open to wild speculations regarding these events, generally termed "conspiracy theories", though this term obscures the crucial distinction between elaborate prospective plots involving many actors (silly in the context of an open society) and retrospective cover-ups that government officials who have made embarrassing mistakes are all too prone to engage in (very realistic and plausible). It is also true that simple prospective plots involving two or three individuals can occur.

Failure to reach a full, shared understanding of major events that have led to unending wars and occupations in the Middle East and Southwest

Asia as well as to the undermining of civil liberties has helped to alienate Americans from their government and media, a triumph for America's enemies. So we must make every effort to establish a clear common interpretation of what actually happened.

Here is an interpretation:

1. The correct diagnosis of President George W. Bush's performance in the run-up to the 9/11/2001 attacks is: *criminal negligence*. He was repeatedly warned that an al Qaeda attack was coming, yet he did nothing to protect the American people, which was his duty. The 9/11 Commission staff covered up Bush's negligence by deliberately failing to ask him the obvious questions: what did he know and when did he know it? It appears that the Democrats on the Commission staff were eager to cover up mistakes Bill Clinton had made in dealing with al Qaeda during his presidency, and so by tacit agreement the Democrats and Republicans on the staff avoided asking tough questions about either Clinton or Bush.

2. Aware of his deep negligence, Bush sought to distract public and media attention by whipping up sentiment for attacking Iraq. Thus Bush's need to distract attention from his negligence became one of the two main reasons for the U.S. attack on Iraq, the other being the efforts of Israel supporters, spearheaded by Deputy Secretary of Defense Paul Wolfowitz, to use U.S. troops against Israel's enemies. These were the necessary and sufficient causes of the attack; all other alleged reasons for the attack were insignificant compared to these. In a crucial way, therefore, the war against Iraq was a *War of Distraction*.

3. The notorious manipulation of intelligence by Wolfowitz, his close associate I. Lewis (Scooter) Libby,[133] and Vice President Dick Cheney in pushing for the Iraq War after 9/11 must raise in turn the question of whether Wolfowitz and Libby, backed by Cheney, had previously sought to obtain a provocation that would lead to a U.S. military intervention

---

[133] Libby became the architect of U.S. policy on torture, with the aim of provoking Muslims to retaliate and thereby entrapping the U.S. in an unending war against Israel's enemies. Vice President Cheney followed Libby's lead. As Cheney staffer Mary Matalin put it, "He is to the vice president what the vice president is to the president." Or less formally, "Scooter is to Cheney as Cheney is to Bush."

against Israel's enemies. In fact, a simple *Curling Conspiracy* (in which Wolfowitz, Libby, and Cheney swept aside any obstacles in the path of the oncoming al Qaeda attack—a kind of Opportunistic Facilitation) makes much more sense than any other explanation of the anomalous failure of the U.S. Government to guard against an amply reported impending attack. According to the serious literature on the 9/11 attacks, Wolfowitz and Libby used at least four techniques: 1) Wolfowitz belittled al Qaeda, which CIA had identified as by far the greatest terrorist threat to the U.S.;[134] 2) he promoted proven phony intelligence about an Iraqi threat;[135] 3) he had a U.S. ambassador who was sounding the alarm about al Qaeda removed;[136] and 4) Libby engaged in delay tactics.[137] White House counterterrorism chief Richard Clarke's characterization of Wolfowitz's actions in his book *Against All Enemies* is especially damning. Clarke correctly considered Wolfowitz an enemy of the American people.

4. The Defense Department's Able Danger intelligence program successfully identified several intending al Qaeda attackers including Mohamed Atta more than a year before the September 11, 2001 attacks. The Defense Department inspector general's report denied the assertions of military officers and others that they recalled Atta's presence on the chart displaying the findings of Able Danger and that they were repeatedly stymied in their efforts to bring their findings to the attention of FBI and others. But this report cannot be taken seriously in view of the indications that the investigation was a cover-up. The Department destroyed extensive evidence and took reprisals against the whistle blowers. The Senate Committee on Intelligence report on Able Danger, which largely echoed the DoD report, was also a cover-up. Deputy National Security adviser Stephen Hadley, the last person known to have a copy of the chart in his possession, has never been questioned about it and may have destroyed it.

---

[134] Richard Clarke, *Against All Enemies* (New York: Free Press, 2004), 231; see also Anthony Summers and Robbyn Swan, *The Eleventh Day: The Full Story of 9/11* (New York: Ballantine Books, 2012), 308

[135] Clarke, 95, 232

[136] Ibid., 233

[137] Summers and Swan, 357; delay tactics are also evident in Clarke, 231-2, 234

5. In 2004 FBI correctly identified Abderraouf Jdey as the Anthrax Mailer of September and October, 2001, and then shoebomber of American Airlines Flight #587 on November 12, 2001. The Jdey identification was covered up because it was terrifically embarrassing: FBI and other U.S. Government agencies had permitted an al Qaeda operative whom FBI had released from detention to carry out two major terrorist attacks. In addition, Bush and Cheney likely feared that tying al Qaeda to the anthrax mailings and the crash of Flight #587 would lead to reinvestigating the run-up to the 9/11 attacks and result in disclosures of the culpability of top administration officials. In the anthrax mailings case, U.S. Army scientist Bruce Ivins seems to have prepared the anthrax before 2001 in order to test vaccines. An Al Qaeda sympathizer appears to have stolen some of this anthrax from a DARPA project at George Mason University. Under pressure from FBI, Ivins committed suicide. Then FBI asserted that he was the Mailer.

In other words, even though presidents, the Congress, and the media have refused or failed to investigate properly or provide satisfactory explanations of these tragic and transformative events, the correct stories, at least in terms of summary characterizations, are knowable. Sufficient information is available to reach "much more likely than not" conclusions, if not "beyond a reasonable doubt" ones; and reaching such conclusions arguably represents a more realistic goal than the likely futile task of seeking to "pry the lids off" cover-ups. In effect, the American people can tell their Government: "Keep your supposedly secret but in fact embarrassing and at times incriminating documents. We already know enough to judge this case." So the problem becomes one of talking things over among ourselves, reaching a shared understanding, making sure that every American learns of it, and insisting that the perpetrators of these shocking and outrageous crimes be brought to justice.

Arriving at an accurate diagnosis is a key step on the path to healing.

Chapter 16

Was Abderraouf Jdey the Anthrax Mailer?

A top secret Canadian Security Intelligence Service report leaked on August 27, 2004 may provide the missing piece of evidence needed to identify the long elusive Anthrax Mailer of 2001.

While confirmation is still lacking, we now have enough shreds of evidence to piece together a theory of the case that resolves key anomalies. In turn, that theory can point us toward where we might find confirmatory evidence.

Figure 33. Abderraouf Jdey

According to the article in Canada's *National Post*[138], Mohammed Mansour Jabarah, a 22-year old Canadian, told interrogators that he had heard from an assistant of Khalid Sheikh Mohammed (KSM), mastermind

---

[138] The article, Bell, Stewart, "Montreal man downed US plane, CSIS told," *National Post*, August 27, 2004, has been removed from the Internet. However, at http://www.scientiapress.com/abderraouf-jdey-shoebombing-flight-587 is a copy of the archived version.

of the 9/11 attacks, that the November 12, 2001 crash of American Airlines Flight #587 in New York was the result of an al Qaeda shoe bomb. The bomber was "Farouk the Tunisian". Newspaper photographs showed him to be Abderraouf Jdey, a 36-year old Montreal-based Canadian of Tunisian origin.

Jdey was one of the seven al Qaeda terrorists listed in the FBI's plea for information from the public in May, 2004. He had emigrated to Canada in 1991, gained citizenship in 1995, and then travelled to Afghanistan where he trained as one of the ten substitutes for the 9/11 attackers. According to KSM, Jdey was slated for pilot training and was to be in the second wave of attacks. Jdey recorded a martyrdom statement in a video later found by American forces in Afghanistan. He returned to Montreal in summer 2001 and was detained by INS and FBI on or around August 16, as was Zacarias Moussaoui. Moussaoui had a computer disk with information on cropdusting (he had previously queried the University of Minnesota about taking a course on cropdusting); Jdey was carrying biology textbooks, according to a 2010 Harvard report. FBI omitted the computer disk from its inventory of Moussaoui's possessions in its court filing, and it did not mention Jdey. Jdey was evidently released. In response to a Freedom of Information request, FBI refused to divulge any information about the detention of Jdey on the grounds that it would constitute an invasion of his privacy.

A Theory of the Case

Al Qaeda had a history of interest in biological weapons. There is evidence that the 9/11 attackers had anthrax in their possession during the months preceding September 11, 2001. They were evidently seeking a way to use a cropduster to spread anthrax over an American city. A medical doctor who treated a future hijacker for a skin lesion stated that the lesion he treated was consistent with one caused by anthrax. A pharmacist reported to FBI that Mohamed Atta, leader of the 9/11 attacks, had sought a remedy for skin irritation on his hands, which were red from the wrists down. An accompanying fellow terrorist sought a remedy for a cough.

If the 9/11 attackers had possessed anthrax, they would have had to hand it off to another al Qaeda operative before September 11. Otherwise the precious vials of anthrax, the first and only weapon of mass destruction that al Qaeda had ever possessed, would have been wasted.

But they wouldn't necessarily trust just any al Qaeda operative to safeguard and perform with the anthrax, and perhaps they knew very few of al Qaeda's sleepers in North America anyway. They would want to give the anthrax to an operative they knew and trusted, one who would use it to the best effect.

Abderraouf Jdey appears to have been exactly such a person. He differed markedly from the nine other 9/11 substitutes. He was older, from a different country of origin, with Canadian citizenship, with semi-sleeper status, and with a clear designation as part of the second wave. He had trained in Afghanistan simultaneously with Mohamed Atta. He was well-enough educated to have been slated for pilot training. In effect, Jdey can be viewed as the counterpart of Atta, as the leader of the second wave of al Qaeda attacks following 9/11.

And he had studied biology at the University of Montreal in his late twenties.

So Jdey was the logical person for Atta to hand off the anthrax to. We can also identify the logical time and place for such a transfer to have occurred.

An especially hard-to-explain anomaly in the hijackers' story has been why Atta and a fellow hijacker travelled from Boston to Portland, Maine on September 10. Taking a feeder flight from Portland to Boston on the morning of September 11 caused Atta nearly to miss his connection, and he and his companion had to pass through security questioning twice rather than once–at a significant added risk of detection.

So Atta must have had a reason to go to Portland that outweighed such risks. The most obvious explanation would be that he had an important meeting on a subject that required face-to-face contact, not just a veiled telephone conversation. A transaction with someone coming from the north, arranged for outside of Boston to lessen the risk of surveillance.

Clearly, Jdey would be a very likely "someone", and handing over the vials of anthrax would furnish a compelling reason for their otherwise risky meeting.

More Anomalies Resolved

If Jdey indeed was the recipient of vials of anthrax in Portland, then subsequent events *could* have followed this course:

While the 9/11 hijackers had sought access to a cropduster to spread the anthrax over an American city, Jdey presumably saw that receiving training at an American flight school was not in the cards after 9/11. So he had to resort to another method of distributing the anthrax. (Another, perhaps more telling explanation is that it was Atta who had the idea of mailing letters and who provided Jdey with a mailing list of targets. Seeking revenge against specific individuals and organizations seems to have been a very characteristic personality trait of Atta.)

Jdey decided to mail the anthrax. The first mailings took place in September soon after the 9/11 attacks. The second mailings, to Senators Daschle and Leahy, occurred in October and included high-quality anthrax. Driving hundreds of miles from Montreal to Trenton to mail the letters made sense because it perfectly disguised Jdey's Canadian base. Jdey's earlier presumed trip to Portland indicates a preference for long cross-border drives to reduce the likelihood of surveillance.

The anthrax letters do not show any obvious Gallicisms betraying that they were from a fluent French-speaker, which Jdey presumably was. But they are consistent with a person who has acquired English as a second language, and there is nothing in them that is inconsistent with Jdey as author. In fact, Jdey is a highly believable author of the anthrax letters. Various objections that have been raised to al Qaeda authorship of the letters can be readily met. For instance, the concept of warning the target that he/she was being attacked was standard al Qaeda procedure, in keeping with an injunction from the Prophet Mohammed.

One of the main characteristics or anomalies of the anthrax mailings case was how remarkably elusive the Mailer was both during his period of activity in autumn, 2001 and thereafter. Despite a massive FBI investigation backed by hundreds of thousands of tips from the American public, the Mailer succeeded in hiding his tracks. Being based in Canada, contrary to every expectation, would nicely explain his elusiveness during his period of activity.

The leaked Canadian intelligence report from 2002 provides a plausible explanation for the lack of information about Jdey's whereabouts since then (as well as for the cessation of the anthrax mailings): Jdey committed suicide on Flight #587 on November 12, 2001.

Why might Jdey be a likely candidate to do this, quite aside from the Jabarah account?

If he was indeed the Anthrax Mailer, he was a hard-headed man of action. Instead of dreaming about impractical schemes of sowing the anthrax in the skies above a city (especially because that would presumably require finding a scientist who could multiply the small samples al Qaeda had, which Atta and others had evidently initially thought feasible), he realized that he had to use it before being captured. And through means (mailing letters) that would minimize the possibility of arrest, which would keep him from fulfilling his pledge to commit suicide in an attack on the enemy. This tactic also enabled him to target the hated Senator Leahy, author of the legislation permitting "renditions" of suspected terrorists to their countries of origin, where they were subjected to torture. (These considerations explain another anomaly–that al Qaeda would use its first weapon of mass destruction in a manner unlikely to cause mass casualties.)

In early November, 2001, Jdey recognized that–as the Anthrax Mailer– he was likely to be arrested at any moment, so he would do well to act on his pledge of martyrdom by turning himself into a shoebomber. The Canadian intelligence report has him leaving Canada in November, though the date is not provided. On November 12 he showed up at Kennedy International Airport and boarded Flight #587. No Canadian passport holders are listed on the final passenger list of Flight #587.

Possessor of many aliases, Jdey presumably had several other passports. A number of the passengers were plausibly francophones; one of them was Jdey.

The cessation of the mailings after October, 2001 following their initial success is another anomaly neatly explained by this account. Yet another anomaly, of course, is that Flight #587 disintegrated and crashed for no apparent reason.

Seeking Confirmation

The scenario sketched out above has the virtue of conforming to the evidence available in a logical manner. Four main perceptions support it: 1) it would powerfully explain Atta's mysterious Portland trip; 2) it would show why the Mailer has proven so elusive and why the mailings ceased (Jdey might also not have revealed to any other al Qaeda operatives that he had the anthrax, so no one would know that he had been the Mailer once he committed suicide.); 3) it fits well the characteristics that caused Jdey to stand out among the substitute hijackers, and indeed that differentiated him from the actual hijackers as well; and 4) FBI's effort to conceal the detention of Jdey along with Zacarias Moussaoui strongly suggests a cover-up.

Of course, there are major gaps in the evidence. There is no direct evidence of a meeting in Portland. The cause of the crash of Flight #587 remains controversial. According to the official inquiry, there was no evidence of an explosion on board. Accounts of eyewitnesses from the ground, however, are highly consistent with a shoe bomb explosion. The explosion could have been small enough to have been masked by wake turbulence from the preceding JAL aircraft. The co-pilot's frantic manipulation of the rudder would thus have been a hopeless attempt to rescue a doomed aircraft.

Still, we don't know when or how Jdey crossed the border. We have no direct evidence that he ever was in Trenton. In short, we don't know a lot that we need to know.

So it is necessary to seek evidence that would confirm, refute, or modify this account. Here are some ways to do so:

- Review the security videos from Kennedy International Airport.
- See if the ticket agents recognize Jdey's photo.
- Check the backgrounds of the likely suspects from the final passenger list.
- Check both Canadian and U.S. border crossing and airport records.
- Test Jdey's apartment for anthrax.
- Test any vehicles he owned or rented for anthrax.

- Interrogate al Qaeda detainees regarding Jdey, shoebombs, and anthrax. Richard Reid, who unsuccessfully attempted a shoebombing just one month after the Flight #587 crash, might know something relevant.
- Hunt through Jdey's background. He was educated in Tunisia as an architectural engineer, then studied geology at the University of Montreal. What kind of biology did he also study in Montreal? Or did he learn about biowarfare in Afghanistan? Did he hold any subsequent job? Had he served in the Tunisian police or army? What kind of a person was he?
- Publicize Jdey and his photo more widely than at present, in hopes of finding further evidence from the public.

The publicly available evidence suggests that Abderraouf Jdey brought down Flight #587 with a shoebomb.

Was he also the Anthrax Mailer? Evidence and logic make him the leading suspect.

A Critical Stage

The original version of this analysis was submitted to FBI in September, 2004. Within a few days of its submission, security for at least some international flights was intensified and included special double checking of shoes. On October 22, 2004 the judge in the Steven Hatfill, M.D. suit said that FBI had told him that its investigation had reached "a critical stage." Around this time FBI stopped providing regular briefings on the investigation to the targets and relatives of victims of the anthrax mailings. Also, the information that Abderraouf Jdey had studied biology at the University of Montreal was added to his FBI public profile after September, 2004; the original version of this analysis had only suggested that Jdey might have had a pertinent education such as in chemical engineering. In other words, in a sense, the Jdey theory proved predictive. Subsequently, FBI removed detailed information about Jdey from its Websites, including the reference to his study of biology.

On April 20, 2005, the U.S. Government announced a new reward of up to $5 million for information on Jdey. In this period FBI's management began to deprive the investigation, led by Richard Lambert from 2002 to 2006, of resources, according to his later suit over retaliation against his whistle blowing.[139]

An isolated report that Jdey entered Turkey in 2002 is evidence contrary to the above account, but it could readily be explained by the use of an altered passport by another al Qaeda operative. Also, as a suicide pledger, Jdey was committed to follow the example of his 9/11 comrades. Failing to do so would have earned him the contempt of his peers. Besides, he would have known that using his real passport in the post-9/11 era was too risky. So this Turkish report merits plenty of skepticism.

Although the above account couches its argument in terms of a search for conclusive proof, in the circumstances of a case where the leading suspect appears to have committed suicide, conclusive proof may never emerge. Therefore, it may be necessary to shift the standard of proof to "preponderance of the evidence". It is very possible that FBI has sufficient evidence for a reasonable person to conclude that, more likely than not, Jdey was the Anthrax Mailer. Indeed, some might conclude that simply on the basis of the evidence and arguments in this analysis.

---

[139] See Lambert's plea in Lambert v. Holder *et al.*, Tennessee Eastern District Court, April 2, 2015: "53. On July 6, 2006, Plaintiff provided a whistleblower report of mismanagement to the FBI's Deputy Director pursuant to Title 5, United States Code, Section 2303. Reports of mismanagement conveyed in writing and orally included: (a) WFO's [FBI's Washington Field Office's] persistent understaffing of the AMERITHRAX investigation;...(j) the FBI's fingering of Bruce Ivins as the anthrax mailer; and, (k) the FBI's subsequent efforts to railroad the prosecution of Ivins in the face of daunting exculpatory evidence. Following the announcement of its circumstantial case against Ivins, Defendants DOJ and FBI crafted an elaborate perception management campaign to bolster their assertion of Ivins' guilt. These efforts included press conferences and highly selective evidentiary presentations which were replete with material omissions....55....Plaintiff continued to advocate that while Bruce Ivins may have been the anthrax mailer, there is a wealth of exculpatory evidence to the contrary, which the FBI continues to conceal from Congress and the American people...."

All other theories of the case (including FBI's weak, 100% circumstantial one) face the severe handicap of having to provide plausible explanations for anomalies that this theory resolves, including above all the outstanding anomaly of Atta's trip to Portland, Maine. FBI's theory provides no plausible explanations for some of these anomalies and only feeble ones for others. In addition, FBI's claim to have cleared all those with access to the anthrax other than Bruce Ivins does not account for the possibility of theft of the anthrax, as discussed below.

For the sake of argument, one could still assume that Jdey was not the Mailer. This would make the evidence and logical connections adduced in the discussion above a mere string of coincidences. Atta's trip to Portland, Jdey's study of biology, his apparent role as leader of the Second Wave, the ways in which he stood out from the hijackers and their substitutes, his high believability as the author of the anthrax letters, FBI's concealment of his detention at the same time as Zacarias Moussaoui, the perfect match in regard to timing, the compelling reasons for his elusiveness, the account of Mohammed Mansour Jabarah—all these would become sheer happenstance.

Hard to believe.

So it is reasonable to think that the answer to "Was Abderraouf Jdey the Anthrax Mailer?" is: more likely than not. Or rather: much more likely than not.

The Origin of the Anthrax

How did al Qaeda gain access to the anthrax? According to attorney Ross Getman, an expert on al Qaeda's biowarfare program, it had opportunities at several university laboratories, including one at George Mason University. In this writer's opinion, going beyond the conclusions of Getman, the most likely route was via a collaborative biodefense research project funded by DARPA and involving Advanced Biosystems, Inc. and what would become George Mason University's National Center for Biodefense and Infectious Diseases. At GMU's Manassas, Virginia facility, Islamic ideologue Ali Al-Timimi, later imprisoned for recruiting American Muslims to fight U.S. forces in Afghanistan, was a graduate student in computational biology with an office around the corner from that of Charles Bailey, Vice President of Advanced Biosystems and former deputy commander of the U.S. Army Medical Research Institute of Infectious Diseases at Fort Detrick in Frederick, Maryland.

The project was using an avirulent Delta strain of anthrax from NIH. However, Bailey may have been the "former deputy commander" who was one of FBI's ultimate four main suspects—presumably meaning that he had obtained a sample of virulent anthrax.

DoD would have wished to devise countermeasures to the alarming technological innovations of the Soviet biowarfare program it learned about from Ken Alibek (whose office was next to Bailey's at GMU), former deputy director of the Soviet program, and other defectors (this explanation appears far more likely than that the U.S. Government itself was running an offensive bioweapons program; biowarfare is antithetical to U.S. interests, whereas it was a major component of Soviet weapons development and strategy). One of these innovations appears to have been a special formulation of anthrax. To devise countermeasures, DoD would have wanted to prepare enhanced anthrax as a vaccine challenge. In a more general sense, ensuring the adequacy of biodefense measures necessitates developing offensive capability to test them.

FBI's theory of the case treats the problem of preparing the anthrax as one of merely purifying and drying spores. But the anthrax in the senators' letters in addition possessed special characteristics that caused individual particles to waft upward spontaneously. It had a high silicon content—reportedly 1.45% in the Leahy letter and possibly higher in the Daschle one, well above natural background levels. And the crude anthrax in the letter to the *New York Post* had a 10% silicon content, impossible to interpret as anything but an addition. Its tin content was 0.65%—far above background level; tin can catalyze the fusion of silicon into a silicone layer.

In its February 15, 2011 report, the National Academy of Sciences identified a bimodal pattern in the letters to the senators in which exceedingly tiny particles, 1.5 microns in diameter on average, were accompanied by clumps larger than 20 microns in diameter. The tiny particles were dramatically smaller than known U.S. and Soviet anthrax; and the particles—which appear to be individual spores—were of a very uniform size. NAS argued that silicon was not added to the senators' letters, because the tiny particles would have spontaneously wafted upward individually on their own. But it does not take into account that silicon could have been added to induce the larger clumps to break apart and disperse also (the 1.5 micron diameter particles constituted only 1/2000 of the Daschle anthrax) or addition of the silicon would have enhanced the dispersal of the tiny particles.

While the silicon collected in the spore coat inside the exosporium, the tiny particles resisted clumping, suggesting the possibility that rigidity caused by the silicon in the coat, changes in electrical or chemical properties caused by the uptake of the silicon, or a hard-to-detect silicon monolayer on the exosporium (microencapsulation) had influenced the interaction of the spores. The NAS report assumes that only silicon on the exosporium would act as a dispersant, but this has not been tested or proven.

It is not clear whether the silicon collected equally in the tiny and the larger particles; whether the tiny particles possessed other characteristics distinguishing them from the larger particles; or whether all spores—individual or clumped—were of the same size.

Preparation and Theft of the Anthrax

The evidence assembled by FBI strongly suggests that U.S. Army scientist Bruce Ivins prepared (processed) the anthrax. But, if this is correct, he does not appear to have done it at USAMRIID. It seems that he would have prepared powdered virulent anthrax at a facility like Southern Research Institute (SRI) in Frederick

Figure 34. Bruce Ivins

that presumably had considerably more appropriate equipment than was available at USAMRIID as well as a Biological Safety Level 3 facility. Patricia F. Fellows, Ivins's closest collaborator at USAMRIID, who later moved to SRI, appears to have been the only one of his close associates who thought that he was the Mailer—perhaps because she knew that he had had access at SRI to the anthrax that showed up in the letters. Fellows, who had expertise in aerosols, was the only current USAMRIID employee to whom FBI's bloodhounds reacted, so she might have collaborated with Ivins in preparing the anthrax.

David Franz, commander of USAMRIID from 1995 to 1998, then retired and became head of the Chemical and Biological Defense Division of SRI until around 2003. Neither Franz (initially responsive to requests for information about aspects of the case but then increasingly evasive) nor any other past or current managers at SRI respond to inquiries about pre-9/11 work on virulent anthrax at SRI. SRI was also subcontractor with Hadron/Advanced Biosystems, the partner with GMU on the DARPA anthrax contract, of which Charles Bailey was co-principal investigator. SRI's role was to perform testing. Franz and Bailey had been at USAMRIID together (possibly Bailey was deputy commander under Franz, but biographical information are lacking).

Therefore, SRI emerges as the most likely place for the anthrax in the letters to have been prepared; and propinquity, seniority, excellent lab skills, expertise with anthrax and vaccine testing, custodianship of the main anthrax flask RMR-1029,[140] and working relationship with DoD entities would make Ivins the most likely preparer, probably assisted by Patricia Fellows.

Judging from evidence (inquiries at airfields regarding cropdusters) suggesting that Mohamed Atta's gang in Florida had obtained the anthrax by February, 2001, Ivins appears to have prepared the anthrax at SRI in a 1998-2000 timeframe. Then, responding to the heightened threat reports in the run-up to the September 11, 2001 attacks, he seems to have taken out samples he had earlier brought to USAMRIID and started testing vaccines, which would explain the upsurge in his hours spent in the hot suite starting in August. This would also explain why, subsequent to the

---

[140] However, the anthrax in the letters differed slightly from that in RMR-1029, which came in 1997 from the U.S. Army's Dugway Proving Ground in Utah. Franz and Bailey should know the origin of the anthrax in the letters and how it came to SRI.

anthrax mailings, he twice swabbed down, then cleaned his lab without authorization.

Franz appears to have provided vials of the powdered anthrax to Bailey without telling Ivins, and Ivins seems to have been allowed to believe that the anthrax at SRI was safely locked in a freezer, so that Ivins assumed that the Mailer was a USAMRIID scientist who had stolen samples of the anthrax from himself.

Around the time of the anthrax attacks, Ivins also developed an infection on his hand that required visits to two doctors and two antibiotics, including doxycycline, the treatment of choice for cutaneous anthrax and the one that was successful. Against regulations, Ivins concealed the infection and treatment from USAMRIID. This information, which appeared in the March 14, 2011 psychiatry group report on Ivins, is hard to interpret as meaning anything but that he had developed cutaneous anthrax from experimenting with powdered virulent anthrax in the hot suite. In other words, at the very time Ivins was later accused by FBI of spending hours at night in the hot suite preparing the anthrax to mail in the letters, in fact he appears to have been testing vaccines to protect the American public from a terrorist anthrax attack.

At GMU, Bailey has remained silent and refers questioners to a university lawyer. The University has "recommended" to noted GMU microbiologist Sergei Popov that he refrain from public discussion of the anthrax case.

Bailey filed a patent application in March, 2001 along with co-principal investigator on the DARPA project Ken Alibek on a method for treating biological samples such as anthrax spores. This method can be characterized as a primarily Soviet technique for preparing cells, with wide commercial potential. It includes repeated references to silica and appears to involve microencapsulation with an ultrathin layer of silica.

Amid lax laboratory and computer security, Al-Timimi seems to have stolen from an unlocked refrigerator small amounts of anthrax of various kinds made from RMR-1029. Al-Timimi then provided the anthrax to Mohamed Atta.

An important implication of this is that al Qaeda in Afghanistan or elsewhere had nothing to do with the anthrax mailings. The attacks were a 100% North American al Qaeda operation. Nor did al Qaeda require any sophistication to prepare the anthrax; all Al-Timimi had to know was that these vials contained virulent anthrax. The transmission route was fairly simple and short: Franz to Bailey to Al-Timimi to Atta to Jdey. Moreover, it seems possible that Jdey did not inform his colleagues in Canada that he had obtained or used the anthrax, so once he committed suicide no one would know that he was the Mailer.

Thus it appears that:

- The special varieties of anthrax were prepared well before the 9/11 attacks and were intended for testing vaccines against realistic threats. The crude anthrax in the letter to the *New York Post* may have been intended as a control to determine how much more effective the refined anthrax was;
- Much more likely than not, Bruce Ivins was the Preparer of the anthrax in the letters (possibly in collaboration with Patricia Fellows). The evidence collected by FBI seems persuasive on this point, though we will not have watertight proof until Fellows, Franz, and Bailey are asked and answer tough questions. At any rate, even if someone else had prepared the anthrax, Ivins was clearly working with it in August through October, 2001. Soon thereafter, Ivins evidently began to hide his role as the (presumed) Preparer. He evidently feared that, if he admitted to having had access to the powdered anthrax or if FBI found evidence that he had had it or was actually working with it in the hot suite at the time of the attacks, FBI would never have believed that he hadn't mailed it, given his lurid psychiatric history and habits, including mailing of false-flag letters. (Despair over ever being able to prove his innocence for these reasons may also have been the motive for his eventual suicide.) In turn, the FBI investigators interpreted his behavior as betraying guilt;
- All of the key, apparently valid pieces of evidence used by FBI and others to identify Ivins as the Mailer—the details of his skin infection, his deletion of his emails in 2001, his unauthorized cleanings of his lab space, and his incorrectly submitted samples of RMR-1029 anthrax (although this is disputed by critics)—can equally apply to an Innocent Preparer of the virulent powdered

anthrax. They show that Ivins likely prepared the anthrax, contrary to what many have argued; but they do not show that he mailed it;

- Ivins appears to have prepared the anthrax at SRI, which would have had the required equipment, supplies, and facilities. He was sufficiently skilled to prepare the powdered anthrax if he had written instructions and/or coaching, presumably available at SRI—or perhaps without either instructions or coaching but with the assistance of Patricia Fellows. Franz and Bailey—neither former bioweaponeers nor bench microbiologists—had presumably accumulated considerable lore from intelligence on foreign programs as well as the old U.S. program about methods for enhancing the delivery of anthrax spores. These could have included a formula for catalyzing silicon with organotin to provide a silicone layer on the spore coat. Thus it appears that the special characteristics of the anthrax reflected the pooled lore of Ivins, Fellows, Franz, and Bailey on how to enhance the effectiveness of powdered virulent anthrax to carry out realistic animal testing of vaccines. This would explain why there has been so much controversy about whether the anthrax was enhanced or "weaponized": it was a halfway-in-between product of one or more savvy individuals who had never made a bioweapon before but had some notions of how to do it;
- DoD, SRI, Hadron, and GMU appear to have concealed highly relevant information from FBI investigators, allowing them to pursue their erroneous theory of the case; and these organizations (and Ivins) may have destroyed any special anthrax remaining after the attacks; and
- The anthrax mailings—carried out for al Qaeda by a Canadian citizen of Tunisian origin based in Montreal and using anthrax prepared for the Department of Defense by a key U.S. Army scientist, then stolen by an American al Qaeda sympathizer—were an inextricable mixture of foreign and domestic elements.

Suppression of Evidence

As for the FBI investigation, one can surmise that FBI found enough further evidence in 2004 successfully to identify Jdey as the Anthrax Mailer and shoebomber of Flight #587. But this finding (to which only a tiny number were privy) would have been exceptionally embarrassing At a time of the highest alert, the Bureau and the rest of the U.S. Government had failed to stop an al Qaeda operative, whose whereabouts were known and who had even been detained, from perpetrating two major attacks.

A previous cover-up of evidence that Flight #587 had been brought down by a terrorist shoebomb is also possible. Lastly and most importantly, President Bush and Vice President Cheney appear to have been eager to avoid finding an al Qaeda anthrax mailer in order to forestall calls to reinvestigate the events of 2001, and specifically the ultra-sensitive question of what had gone on at the top level of the U.S. Government in the run-up to the 9/11 attacks. At any rate, there seems to have been a conspiracy to suppress all evidence regarding Jdey and to find some other suspect, which led eventually to the of-necessity invalid case against Bruce Ivins.

*****

Now that we have gone through the theory of the case, it makes sense to delve more deeply into FBI's case against Ivins and into the various objections that have been raised against an al Qaeda interpretation of the case.

FBI v. Bruce Ivins: The Missing Pieces

There are two sides to every story. Judges rightly admonish juries to check out both sides before coming to a conclusion. Our entire system of adversarial justice is built on this principle. But under surveillance by FBI in the 2001 anthrax mailings case, U.S. Army scientist Bruce Ivins committed suicide. So only one side got to tell its version of the story.

Upon closing the case on February 19, 2010, FBI issued an *Amerithrax Investigative Summary* that concludes that Ivins was the anthrax mailer. The *Summary* contains serious errors as well as minor ones. It also omits crucial information. So, to ensure a fair outcome, we need to look at it through the eyes of a defense attorney, to make sure that the American people can check out both sides of the story before coming to a conclusion.

First, let's take a critical look at the arguments FBI makes. Then we can turn to the omissions.

Seven Flaws

There are seven main flaws in the Summary's arguments:

1. FBI claims that it has direct evidence that Ivins mailed the letters, not just circumstantial evidence. But its direct evidence turns out to be that Ivins was the custodian of the purported source of the anthrax used, flask RMR-1029. That is in a sense direct evidence, but since the Bureau itself admits that the anthrax used in the case could have come from any of the hundreds of scientists who had access to samples from RMR-1029, it is not exclusive evidence. Yet in its common meaning, "direct" evidence is tied exclusively to the accused individual, so ostensibly direct evidence such as the RMR-1029 flask actually becomes a kind of circumstantial evidence in reference to Ivins or any other scientist who prepared the anthrax. Characterizing the evidence as entirely circumstantial seems a good deal more accurate than FBI's misleading characterization, and it provides a powerful reason for skepticism about FBI's entire case. There's not a shred of direct evidence that can be pinned on Ivins, and on nobody else. Besides, analysis of the anthrax in the letters suggests that it was not

derived from RMR-1029 but rather was its cousin that came from somewhere else than USAMRIID. If Ivins worked with it, he presumably had been given access to it to carry out a special project.

2. One of FBI's key arguments is that Ivins spent extra hours at night in the "hot suites" at USAMRIID, Fort Detrick preparing the anthrax just before the mailings of September and October, 2001. But his calendar and related documentation show that he had scheduled duty to check on a test of an anthrax vaccine on scores and perhaps hundreds of animals on those nights.

3. FBI argues that Ivins had the equipment and skills to prepare the anthrax in the letters to the senators. Critics have voiced objections, including that USAMRIID did not possess the proper equipment and that preparing powdered spores would have required far too much time. At a minimum, preparing the anthrax and then cleaning the equipment would clearly have required a good deal of time and effort—hard to hide from co-workers. However, there are good reasons to believe that in fact Ivins *did* prepare the anthrax; but that he did so a year or two earlier for a Department of Defense project to provide realistically enhanced variants in order to test vaccines. Moreover, he did not do it at USAMRIID, but rather at another Biosafety Level 3 laboratory in Frederick—and he did not mail the anthrax letters.

4. While Ivins had many long-standing quirks and obsessions, he plainly deteriorated in the last year of his life under FBI pressure and excessive intake of alcohol and medications. FBI's effort to use evidence of pathological tendencies from this period to portray his earlier state of mind and behavior seems very unpersuasive. Moreover, a key witness who provided lurid testimony regarding Ivins during his last year was his addictions counselor, Jean Duley. Duley, who described herself as a former motorcycle gang member and hard drug user, had repeated arrests for DUI.[141] Likewise, Ivins's counselor, Judith McLean, who reported his plan in 2000 to poison his former lab technician if she lost her soccer match, is the author of a book in which she vaunts her psychic powers, discusses her out-of-body experiences, and communicates with a megalithic French stone. Duley's and McLean's accounts of Ivins may or

---

[141] *The Washington Post*, August 6, 2008

may not be accurate, but they hardly rate as credible witnesses; both might well have put a spin on their reports. In addition, the March 23, 2011 report on Ivins by psychiatrists and others misinterpreted his psychological profile. (They claimed to be independent, but in fact the director of the panel, Gregory Saathoff, had consulted in the investigation at a critical junction.) A lifelong, energetic emitter of ideations of violence, Ivins never once caused physical harm to another person. Scores or even hundreds of ideations; zero acts. This extreme disproportion suggests that Ivins had a powerful inhibition against doing physical harm to others, presumably derived from observing as a child his mother's (provoked by taunting) assaults on his father. Thus to send virulent anthrax by mail would have violated a taboo. It would have been totally out of character. He was psychologically incapable of doing physical harm to any other person. Indeed, when he was trapped, desperate, and angry at the end, he went and told his ideations of violent revenge against perceived enemies to his whole therapy group so that somebody would be sure to stop him.

5. FBI's claim that the language of the letters resembled that of Ivins could apply to hundreds of other possible writers of the letters. Its effort to find evidence in them of Ivins's use of a hidden genetic code seems fanciful, is certainly unproven, and is lacking in probative value. A person interviewed by FBI about the writing in the letters stated "the more you look the more unclear it is."[142]

6. FBI repeatedly assumes that the preparer and the mailer of the anthrax were the same person, but there is telling evidence (see below) that they were not.

7. The statements and actions of Ivins that FBI claims were signs of a guilty conscience can just as readily be interpreted as evidence of an innocent man's well-founded fear that, if FBI found evidence that he had prepared the anthrax powder, it would never believe that he had not mailed it because of his lurid psychiatric history. His entire pattern of behavior fits perfectly the pattern of someone who prepared the anthrax, but did not mail it.

---

[142] http://foia.fbi.gov/filelink.html?file=amerithrax/847547.pdf, 22

The Missing Pieces

While the seven flaws in FBI's case against Ivins already include important omissions (e.g., of Ivins's scheduled duty to check the animal experiment), the critical issues that are not dealt with in the *Summary* are arguably at least as important as the flawed arguments it contains. Let's start with the lesser omissions and move up to the greater ones.

1. Ivins was a much more many-sided, social, and in this sense normal person than FBI's *Summary* would lead one to believe. He played the piano in church, played and sang in a Celtic band, composed songs for departing colleagues, was an expert juggler who taught kids how to juggle, and was involved in a number of groups such as Red Cross. He was married and was the father of two adopted children. He had relationships with dozens of co-workers, ranging from professional to quasi-intimate. So in spite of the quirks and obsessions that FBI dwells on, Ivins was clearly an active contributor to his community, in addition to being a hard-working, productive scientist.
2. Even in regard to Ivins's quirks and obsessions, FBI withholds a full accounting from the public on the grounds that they are not relevant to the anthrax mailings. Did deviations from normality include some that were highly embarrassing to Ivins, ones that he would have hated to become public knowledge in the course of a trial? Would they explain his fears of being (incorrectly) targeted as the anthrax mailer, or his suicide? Could he have been eager to protect the identity of any partners? Ivins was perhaps open to blackmail. He might indeed have felt guilty about something else that FBI does or does not know about.
3. Omitted from FBI's *Summary* are Ivins's lab notebooks, paper and computer files, and information about meetings, phone conversations, and other work he was doing in September and October, 2001. These sources may well contain details on animal experiments and other activities that undermine FBI's case. In particular, FBI has withheld Ivins's email messages on September 17, the date on which he was supposed to have mailed the first letters in Trenton, New Jersey. One must wonder whether the time the messages were sent would make it difficult or impossible to

drive to Trenton. The rationale of withholding sensitive content does not apply because that can all be redacted, leaving just the time. In addition, FBI has withheld several of Ivins's laboratory notebooks. FBI also has never released traditional forensic evidence, such as on the photocopiers Ivins had access to.

4. The February 15, 2011 National Academy of Sciences report on the scientific aspects of the case left many questions unanswered. The NAS chose not to review classified information, in part because FBI refused to provide information to the committee on key subjects. Nor did NAS cover all the investigative aspects of the scientific evidence. For instance, FBI has not identified at Fort Detrick the *Bacillus subtilis* strain contaminant found in the earlier letters, suggesting that the anthrax was prepared elsewhere. More generally, the lax laboratory and computer security in regard to anthrax at laboratories other than Fort Detrick in the pre-September 11, 2001 era needs much more examination. FBI's failure to address these and other investigative questions that relate to the scientific aspects of the case represent significant omissions.

5. Lastly and most importantly, the *Summary* dismisses al Qaeda in a few sentences. That is clearly unacceptable. An array of evidence and logic suggests that al Qaeda stole the anthrax and mailed the letters. The American people deserve a much fuller accounting.

Summing Up

Now that we have heard the other side of the story, the case looks quite different from what FBI claims it to be. However, we should not rule out the possibility that the Department of Defense and its contractors concealed highly relevant information about the case from the FBI investigators, allowing them to pursue an erroneous theory of the case. At any rate, given FBI's flawed arguments and omissions of critical information, its case against Bruce Ivins should not persuade anyone interested in getting to the bottom of the anthrax mailings story. Something is very wrong here.

Objections, Objections

Now let us consider the objections to an al Qaeda theory.

Amid the twists, turns, and baffling uncertainties of the 2001 anthrax mailings case, many observers have managed to hold fast to one conviction: that the anthrax letters can't possibly have been the work of al Qaeda. But are they right? One way to find out would be to identify the actual Mailer. That may prove easier than often thought—if one looks in the right place. Another approach would involve analyzing each of the objections to determine its merits. Let's try that.

1. Many observers hold that the kind of anthrax found in some of the letters clearly comes from the flask of virulent anthrax maintained by Bruce Ivins at the United States Army Research Institute of Infectious Diseases in Frederick, Maryland. So how would it get into the hands of al Qaeda? One answer: some 300 scientists had access to this anthrax, including those in universities and biotechnology companies. In the lax pre-9/11 security environment, various al Qaeda-sympathizer scientists therefore had plenty of opportunities to steal the anthrax, as detailed by researcher Ross Getman.[143] It wasn't particularly difficult. A second answer: the attack anthrax contained certain minor components that were not present in Ivins's flask, in a way that suggests that the attack anthrax came from a different source.

2. Careful analysis of the anthrax letters, many claim, shows them to be fakes concocted by someone who made them look like something al Qaeda would write. For instance, a real al Qaeda operative would have started the letters with an invocation to Allah. But this assumes that al Qaeda types are cut from the same cloth, which is demonstrably false. They come from all over the Muslim world, including from sophisticated westernized cultures. While such operatives might start with an invocation, they might well not.

3. Another very common objection arises from the advice in the letters to take "Penacilin". No al Qaeda operative would have warned his victims and provided the correct antidote, it is felt. But in fact the Prophet enjoined

---

[143] See https://caseclosedbylewweinstein.wordpress.com/.

his followers to warn their enemies when they were going to attack them. In this case, because the Mailer was unable to warn his targets beforehand, at least he told them it was anthrax and indicated the remedy. At any rate, the reference to penicillin is not unequivocal evidence.

4. A favorite objection is that al Qaeda would not have wasted the anthrax on a few recipients of the letters. It would have tried to dispense the anthrax from a cropduster or release it in a subway. In fact, Mohammed Atta and his gang of intending hijackers, who appear to have been handling anthrax in Florida, did seek a cropduster but were frustrated in their efforts. Moreover, mailing poisoned letters has a secure place in the repertoire of clandestine organizations in the Middle East. And Atta, who may well have drawn up the list of addresses for the letters, had a strong need for vengeance that would make the killing of a single person in an anthrax letter attack worthwhile, as long as it was the right person. As with many other "al Qaeda would (or wouldn't) have" objections, this line of reasoning relies on untenable assumptions about how al Qaeda members think as well as about the constraints (e.g., the threat of imminent arrest) under which they operate.

5. A more serious objection is that, if al Qaeda indeed did possess anthrax, it would not stop with a single flurry of minor mailings. It would attack again and again. Yet it has not. Here the explanation has only slowly emerged. It is that the anthrax used in the 2001 mailings seems never to have left North America. Rather than being the product of an al Qaeda biowarfare program, the anthrax was prepared in a U.S. Government-associated lab in an effort to test vaccines against advanced Soviet-era anthrax, then stolen from a North American university or biotech business lab, prepared for use here, and inserted into the envelopes without any of it having been saved or shipped to al Qaeda's headquarters in Afghanistan. So when the last letter was sent, al Qaeda had no more anthrax.

6. Another rather common objection holds that targeting liberal Democratic Senators Daschle and Leahy made no sense for al Qaeda. But Leahy was an arch-enemy, in al Qaeda's eyes, because he had sponsored the rendition law that enabled U.S. agencies to return captured operatives to their countries of origin, where they would be subject to torture and possible execution. That Leahy was a liberal Democrat meant nothing

compared to rendition. So the fact that one letter was addressed to Leahy constitutes another piece of evidence that the attacks were from al Qaeda.

7. Still another argument is that, if al Qaeda had carried out the attacks, it would have claimed credit for them. Not necessarily. Sometimes al Qaeda might choose to remain silent in order to mislead the enemy. In this case, such a tactic might have succeeded royally, considering the confusion, quasi-paranoia, and failure to come to closure we have experienced. However, it is also possible that an al Qaeda perpetrator carried out the anthrax attacks without informing headquarters and then committed suicide. So one very likely outcome of the case could have been that neither al Qaeda nor the U.S. Government would ever know for a certainty that the attack had come from an al Qaeda operative.

Sobering Conclusions

Thus, upon closer examination the seemingly unanswerable objections to the al Qaeda theory shrink or vanish altogether. However, it must be acknowledged that certain of them (#3 and 5) looked very persuasive and required special interpretation to overcome. It should therefore not surprise us that some very smart people have been misled.

And that leads to sobering conclusions.

Although the impact of one person mistakenly thinking that al Qaeda could not have perpetrated the anthrax attacks seems small, cumulatively tens or hundreds of thousands of such mistakes have powerfully contributed to the failures of the investigation. The conviction that the Mailer was domestic led to unfounded suspicions about Steven Hatfill and others while permitting the media to get away with focusing on the Hatfill court cases instead of on the crime and its investigation. This conviction also contributed to the very dubious identification of Bruce Ivins as the Mailer. And it has kept observers from seeking out information on the al Qaeda theory of the case that is readily available on the Internet.

These errors also appear to have permitted the Bush Administration to cover up the embarrassing Jdey story and thereby to carry out its policies with much more credibility and public support than it deserved.

Lastly, it wasn't just a question of uninformed people getting things wrong. As noted above, some very sophisticated, highly informed, keen-eyed observers made these mistakes, and some of the misleading thinking seemed eminently sensible—reminders of our limitations in dealing with terrorism. Terrorists seek to exploit our weaknesses and especially to activate our capacity for inflicting damage on ourselves. In the anthrax mailings case, they certainly seem to have succeeded.

Chapter 17

Conclusion

As varied as our subject matter may seem, we can still make plenty of analytical use of it! Besides, our subjects are hardly lacking in intrigue and importance: the origin of the terrestrial planets, the triggering cause of the five great mass extinctions, the Earth's knack for turning over when approached by a celestial body, the greatest ongoing case of Scientific Rejectionism, the assassination of John F. Kennedy, the 2001 terrorist attacks.... If we can solve even a few of these puzzles, then we have made the case for a past that is more knowable than is often acknowledged. And each time we resolve some anomaly, we deepen our understanding of the past, making us better equipped to handle other such anomalies as well as the exigencies of the present and future.

So let us sift through what we have learned and try to extract fitting conclusions. But first, I need to fulfill the promise in Chapter 1 of a list of eight new reasons to accept Velikovsky's Venus and Reversing Earth theories:

1. The explanation that Venus was pulled from the outer solar system by Jupiter's gravity, heated up, and gained a cometary tail

seems far more persuasive than the notion that it exploded from Jupiter itself.

2. We now have two newly interpreted, powerfully descriptive myths: 1) the Metis (Venus) myth in which, turned into a fly, she flew into Zeus' mouth and gave birth to Athena, who (in the Athena myth) emerged from his head; and 2) the sequential version of the Archer Yi myth, which so neatly records a ten-day inversion of Earth, even to the point of a comet's tail turning each day opposite from the changing direction of the Sun. We can see with Archer Yi that the initial interpretation required knowing that there was a sequential version, being aware of Venus' vermilion, double/curved tail, and knowing about inversions. So it wasn't at all simple. But now that the interpretation is available, any intelligent ten-year old, as well as any scientific critic of Velikovsky, can understand it. And be able to understand the Metis and Athena myths, too. We now can see that the wholesale dismissal of ancient myths as sources of scientific insight is indefensible.

3. There is a simple explanation of the slow retrograde (but swiftly changing to prograde) rotation of Venus, an outstanding anomaly of planetary science: it is the result of tidal locking to Jupiter.

4. Jupiter's gravitational pull turned Venus into an ovoid, as depicted in ancient iconography. This in turn opens our eyes to many instances of Venus-related ovals (obviously, not every oval referred to Venus; we must consider the context) and thus improves our knowledge of ancient culture.

5. Many new instances of iconography, Venus sites, and effigies fill out the framework of the Venus theory; and telling linguistic matches (*A Fena*, *Bos eidon*) add to the picture.

6. We now have a better date (shortly before 2500 BC) for the first approach of Venus, one that matches evidence from Egypt (the Great Sphinx, Hathor with ovoid Venus in her horns alongside Menkaure) and the great reconstruction of Stonehenge.

7. We know the approximate dates of the four inversions of Earth during approaches of Venus. Here we need to do more research to determine whether the four inversion catastrophes were equally

disastrous, or whether for some reason they differed. Those of ca 2200 and 1210 BC seem to have had a greater impact, perhaps because Venus came closer to Earth. So perhaps the four inversions were not all ten days in length. Also, the ca 1628 BC date of the second inversion is the most provisional of the four and requires more research to pin down.

8. We now have two theories that derive from the Venus and Reversing Earth theories. The Outer Solar System Origin of the Terrestrial Planets (OSSO) generalizes the Venus theory, adding much corroborating evidence. OSSO explains the origin of the Pacific Basin as the result of the separation of Mars from Earth by Jupiter's gravity upon passage of Terramars into the inner solar system. In turn, the Martian Theory of Mass Extinctions (MTME) combines tidal destruction caused by planetary approaches with rapid inversion from the Theory of the Reversing Earth to help explain the devastation on Earth as well as the remarkable evidence of disruption on the surface of Mars. These theories provide mutual support and can be considered components of a general tidal theory of the terrestrial planets that outperforms existing *ad hoc* hypotheses, assumption-bound mathematical modeling, and *in situ* uniformitarianism. These theories also lend themselves to testing.

Thus we can see that the task of the critics has become a rather overwhelming one if their goal is to deny any validity to Velikovsky's two great theories. In turn, we can shift from combatting their views toward a further investigation of the theories and related subjects. We should not waste valuable time and energy responding to incorrigible deniers. If they choose to continue to reject and denigrate Velikovsky, they will be consigning themselves to the sidelines.

While this book takes the view that the Venus and Reversing Earth theories constitute Velikovsky's main achievements, we should not rule out the possibility that other claims he made have merit. We need also to investigate the many findings that Velikovsky's followers have made. Often spoken of slightingly as Velikovskians, these researchers have spent decades exploring the highways and byways of science and ancient history. With the passage of time, it would seem better to term them adherents of the Venus theory, thereby according Velikovsky proper respect, but ensuring that their contributions are not subsumed under Velikovsky's name. In effect, we can move beyond the Velikovsky controversy.

We need to take a fresh look at those features of ancient history that the Venus and Reversing Earth theories illuminate, including myths, iconography, archaeoastronomy sites, building orientations, and the Bible. These theories teach us about the ancients themselves, and certain findings may clue us in to other new scientific and historical insights. We also can assess with better understanding the widespread practice of human sacrifice. From the perspectives of both climate change research and historical developments, moreover, it is useful to have in Venus a very clear trigger of the Bronze Age catastrophes and another mechanism—the four inversions—that explains the features of the worst catastrophes. We can also see that, after things had calmed down by 600 BC, cultural amnesia gave an opening to the cross-civilizational 6th-century religious and philosophical revolution.

Lastly, the Velikovsky case and the findings that have emerged from it have implications for science in general. Scientific modeling of the *ad hoc* Giant Impact hypothesis of the origin of the Moon evidently proved far too adaptable to the circumstances—and far too seductive to many researchers and science writers. This suggests, in turn, that mathematical models of the interactions of the terrestrial planets need a thorough revamping to rid them of uniformitarian assumptions.

Now that we have specifically addressed the Velikovsky-related chapters in this book, let us move on to the other chapters and to a broader consideration of major themes and conclusions.

The Trojan Origin of Roman Civilization

TORC rests on three assumptions that leap beyond the evidence. In my discussion I assumed what was to be proved by positing that the Trojans spoke a Ural-Altaic language. I simply postulated that the Trojans occupied both sides of the Straits. And, without a shred of direct evidence,

I hypothesized that the Greeks won the Trojan War by means of a naval blockade. A fourth assumption, that the Trojans on the European shore retreated to Italy, followed from the other three. Clearly, I was hoping that the weight of evidence and logic subsequently adduced would make the original assumptions seem valid. So, if TORC is correct, then we have an example of using some risky assumptions to reach a knowable piece of history. In other words, assumptions that initially seemed risky became less so once we saw the rest of the argument.

TORC can nicely illuminate a common trait of conspiracies or conspiracy theories. Conspiracies come in various shapes and sizes, but perhaps the most common is the cover-up. Cover-ups are retroactive and involve substituting a concocted story for what actually happened. A few people in the right positions can get them going. And they can become such a part of shared understanding that to question them exposes one to the risk of marginalization and even retaliation.

As we saw in Chapter 10, the Etruscans covered up the embarrassing failure of their ancestors on the European side of the Straits to fight in the Trojan War, as well as their subsequent escape to Italy. Their tale of Rome's founding by Trojans coming by sea entered Roman history and literature, managing to mislead people for more than two thousand years. For their part, the Romans pretended that the Etruscan conquest and domination of Rome for several centuries entailed nothing more than a few Etruscan kings, and that the quisling patricians were actually upstanding Roman patriots whose greatest accomplishment was to rid Rome of the Etruscan kings.

These ancient cover-ups, and counterparts in the recent past, remind us that efforts to avoid embarrassment play a large role in the writing and rewriting of history. They also suggest that, of the many types of conspiracy theories, the charge of a cover-up is the most likely to be true.

Other conspiracy theories can range far and wide, and they can multiply endlessly, as we see from the Kennedy assassination. Yet the chances that a random theory of that case is right must be very low—all but one of them are wrong! And perhaps all of them, if one accepts the Lone Gunman account. Yet the possibility of a cover-up in such circumstances, or even deep in the past, as with TORC, remains significant.

Lastly, TORC affords yet another illuminating example, this one in regard to an appeal to good sense. When I mentioned to a Greek archaeologist that Dorian and Troyan were the same word in different languages, she immediately denied it. Only after I noted that all of my students understood this did she desist. But of course that's no proof, which raises the question of how one can prove things that appear obvious. In this book, in regard to myths, I use the appeal to an intelligent ten-year old's understanding. But that's not a proof either! So we seem to be left with a vague notion of a given argument making "good sense" that anyone (at least ten and older, and intelligent) should grasp. Good sense comes perilously close to the common sense that has so often failed in science, so we need to tread warily here. But ultimately we have to rely on good sense and reason in persuading our listeners to accept certain arguments. If they refuse to acknowledge such a very reasonable point at issue, we might do well to find other listeners.

Key Mistakes in the World Wars

Chapter 11 on strategy in the World Wars moves us into What if? history, and it, too, contains important theoretical conclusions. The more we examine the decisions of Germans and Japanese, the more we see that their own errors, and thus their own leaders, made winning the wars much more difficult. Kaiser Wilhelm and Adolf Hitler were notorious mistake-makers. And Generals Hindenburg and Ludendorff made their share of blunders in the second half of World War I. These wars might have had very different outcomes had even normally competent leaders been in charge.

We may also draw a second conclusion from the Japanese case: that the stark logic of warfare requires mind-bending, against-the-grain decisions. No matter how unlovable or even detestable (as well as remote) Nazi Germany was to the Japanese, they had no viable option other than to abandon their own imperial strategy and throw everything they had into supporting Germany.

Thus in these cases consideration of alternative history makes the history we know a bit more understandable.

Carroll Quigley

While paranoid right wingers viewed Carroll Quigley's account of the role of the Anglo-American Establishment as evidence of deep conspiracy, other observers saw it more as a discussion of how a corporate elite sought to orchestrate developments in a business-friendly—but relatively benign—fashion. Quigley himself approved of many of the goals of the Establishment. He pointed out, though, that their efforts to ensure peace in the lead-up to World War II were naïve, and their power and accomplishments fell far short of their aspirations. He also sharply condemned militaristic, xenophobic forces in American society.

Still, some observers came to look askance at him because he was a source for conspiracy theorists. Also, Quigley's rhetoric worked well in an undergraduate classroom but could be misinterpreted when put into print. The ambiguity of the Establishment's machinations also played a role: many of its activities looked like everyday special-interest lobbying, yet some could well be rated conspiratorial—influencing behind the scenes the selection of presidential candidates, scheming to get the U.S. into World War I on the side of the Allies, etc.

For our purposes, Quigley's analysis of the Anglo-American elite, based on his research in the papers of the Round Table group and his analysis of leading American financial groups and behind-the-scenes maneuvering, provides a deeper look into the forces influencing history than we could get from a mere recounting of events and personalities.

Quigley resembled Velikovsky as a prescient, interdisciplinary thinker.

The KGB and Kennedy

The Kennedy assassination reminds us that myth and taboo play roles in modern history as well as in ancient. Here myth refers not to some meaningful message encoded in a story, but rather to the Kennedy legend, the magical sense of a youthful, handsome, energetic, patrician statesman who would lead America into a bright new era. Taboo refers to the media's suppression of his womanizing. Now that we have a more chastened view of both the myth and the reality beneath the taboo, we can assess the man and his role in a more dispassionate fashion.

Meanwhile, the multitudinous theories of the Kennedy assassination have not surprisingly attracted debunkers. While we should be skeptical of professional skeptics who debunk in a rush to judgment based on slender research, Vincent Bugliosi and Gerald Posner are serious debunkers who performed careful research to show that dozens of theories of the case did not hold water. Unfortunately, as we have seen, Posner (who was followed in this by Bugliosi) incorrectly credited the denial by Yurii Nosenko, the most reliably informative Soviet defector, of KGB involvement with Lee Harvey Oswald. Posner did not realize that Nosenko had no access to the third department of the KGB, which dealt with foreign affairs and had been involved with Oswald.

No doubt, these lawyer-debunkers should have noticed what tens of millions of Americans did—that Jack Ruby's shady persona and murder of Oswald reeked of conspiracy. So they should have refrained from insisting on a Lone Gunman theory that blamed Oswald, and instead they should have realized that the anomaly of Jack Ruby suggested that their debunking had a hole in it somewhere. At any rate, we can be grateful to them for clearing out the underbrush.

In retrospect, we can see that the conspiracy researchers were correct to see possible links to Cuba: the KGB appears to have had the Cubans activate their asset Jack Ruby. They were also right to suspect that other murders were connected to the Kennedy assassination, though some became too enthusiastic in their ascriptions. In general, the researchers (except Pacepa) went wrong in ignoring the KGB and minimizing the linkage between the Cuban Missile Crisis and the assassination.

The 2001 Cover-ups

The events of 2001 feature several traits that need special attention. First, like the combination of Cuban Missile Crisis, Kennedy assassination, and murder of Mary Meyer, they require us to demarcate the problem area correctly. Here we have to ask the question of whether other events after the 9/11 attacks were follow-on al Qaeda attacks. Failure to ask led to poor analysis. But that outcome was connected to a second factor: that American news editors have been running scared of the 9/11 attacks ever since. They seem to sense, or know, that something profoundly shocking and embarrassing was going on inside the U.S. Government in the run-up to 9/11. So they won't touch the central question of the roles of top members of the George W. Bush administration with a ten-foot pole. In effect, we see again the presence of a taboo.

That failure has opened the door to all sorts of wild speculations. As with the Kennedy assassination, many members of the public correctly smelled a conspiracy, even if they did not know exactly what it was.

Meanwhile, the events of 2001 also were marked by a third feature: supporters of the administration used the rapid proliferation of conspiracy theories to brand all 9/11 critics as nutty "conspiracy theorists". Journalists and many others became leery of any theory, no matter how well founded, that challenged the standard version, an allergy to anything smacking of conspiracy. That meant that the seemingly reasonable al Qaeda theories of the crash of Flight #587 and the anthrax mailings entered a limbo from which they have not yet emerged. Anyone proposing them was quickly branded a conspiracy theorist, and not just by administration supporters.

What high U.S. officials were doing in the run-up to the 9/11 attacks, as we saw in Chapter 15, can best be characterized as a Curling Conspiracy involving Paul Wolfowitz, I. Lewis Libby, and Vice President Cheney. They spotted al Qaeda's planning for an attack and raced out ahead of it, sweeping aside obstacles in its path. This conspiracy included elements of both Let It Happen on Purpose (LIHOP) and Make It Happen on Purpose (MIHOP), which helps explain why both arguments appeared among the 9/11 Truth researchers. Three aspects complicated analysis. First, the Curling Conspiracy took place amid a fog of intelligence about possible terrorist attacks that made it hard to determine what exactly was going on. In a speech at West Point in June 2001, Wolfowitz pointed to the Pearl Harbor attack as such an episode; this is perhaps best interpreted as a kind of boasting. Second, the actions of Wolfowitz and Libby were either behind the scenes or deliberate failures to act that were hard to pin down, while everything Cheney did was behind the scenes. Such subtle or hidden criminal acts would not be altogether easy to prove in court. (In parallel fashion, the KGB's putative suggestion of assassination to Oswald was marked by the same subtlety and opacity, and it would make detecting the KGB's role very difficult. Both cases involved a kind of opportunistic facilitation.) Third, the entire notion of senior U.S. Government officials cold-bloodedly *helping* a major terrorist attack against the United States to succeed, in order to provoke a response and thereby entrap the country into ongoing wars against the enemies of another country, is truly shocking and outrageous, and thus not initially easy for many to believe.

The Anthrax Mailings Case

While the 2001 anthrax mailings were overshadowed by the dramatic mass casualty terrorist attacks of 9/11, they deserve careful consideration as the first terrorist attack with a weapon of mass destruction. They also occasioned the largest criminal investigation in American history. As we saw in Chapter 16, that investigation turned into a cover-up that led to the suicide of an innocent U.S. Army scientist, who was then falsely blamed for the mailings. Thus there were two crimes: the mailings themselves and the cover-up orchestrated by the president and vice president of the United States.

The technical nature of a biological attack significantly complicated the investigation, though it eventually afforded valuable insights into the two crimes. It also gave a great boost to the development of bioforensics and of biosecurity, which has become much stricter than in the lax days before 2001.

The anthrax mailings case was complex. Many questions needed answering. Who mailed the letters and why? Who prepared the letters, why, and where? Was the Preparer the Mailer? If not, how was the anthrax transmitted? What explains the characteristics of the attack anthrax? How to interpret the letters and the choice of targets? Why was the seemingly obvious suspect, al Qaeda, ignored or dismissed? What other events and developments might have been connected to the mailings? How to explain the stages and conclusion of the investigation, as well as the role of alleged Mailer Bruce Ivins? How would a skillful attorney have defended him? If there was a cover-up, who ordered it, who carried it out, and why? A satisfactory theory would have to answer all these questions and show how all the pieces fit into a coherent story. As with the origin of the terrestrial planets, an explanation that forms part of a general theory accounting for a wide range of phenomena can outperform an *ad hoc* hypothesis.

*****

Now that we have discussed the main subjects in the book, let us turn to more general conclusions.

Objections and More Objections!

While in principle a proponent of any theory or stance should sincerely try to answer every objection, we have to realize that objections are all-too-easy to make. Any competent lawyer or scientist should be able to come up with a fistful of them. Also, at times people pose objections as a substitute for actually investigating the proposition under consideration. A few of Velikovsky's critics had never read *Worlds in Collision*, and all too often objectors seem too busy to read even an article on a topic. They also frequently underestimate the depth of knowledge of a researcher who has spent years dealing with a subject that the objectors have spent two minutes on. For instance, a critic once dismissed the Jdey theory of the anthrax mailings case in a single sentence on the grounds that it would have been impossible for FBI to keep a cover-up to just a few insiders. How did he know that? It was just a supposition he had, yet it allowed him to sweep all the evidence pointing to al Qaeda and specifically to Jdey under the carpet.

Sometimes, as we have seen, objections rely on a Parameter Game (often unintended), as in the Velikovsky case but also in the objection to the Martian Theory of Mass Extinctions about Mars lacking the mass to exert a sufficient gravitational pull on Earth. That was simply a question of adjusting the distance parameter.

Objections can also, as discussed in Chapter 1, constitute an Objection Game that resembles the Allegation Game often seen in law courts. When an attorney shows an allegation to be groundless, then he or she needs to appeal to the judge to stop the game, saying "*Falsus in uno, falsus in omnibus.*" If the opposing side has been shown to have manufactured one phony allegation, how can we trust any other allegation it makes? In regard to scientific or historical objections, this approach doesn't work so well, partly because there is no judge and partly because the objections may very well be sincerely made and altogether genuine, just wrong. Still, putting forward the concept of an Objection Game can serve to clue the observers (the jury!) in to what is going on.

Another common mistake objectors make is to drop too quickly the elephant-in-the-living-room suspect. This holds for the Kennedy assassination (the KGB) and the anthrax mailings (al Qaeda). And it also holds for the Venus theory. Velikovsky had adduced plenty of evidence and arguments pointing to Venus. His supporters found more. Recent findings reported in this book show that a lot more remained to be found, typically hiding in plain sight, but requiring the right approach to identify. And no doubt there are still others to be identified. So his critics needed to ask whether Venus and eventually Mars indeed had caused the catastrophes (*something* must have caused them, and no other explanation made sense), but in a somewhat different way than Velikovsky had suggested.

Thus we have to look skeptically on objections, especially if they are too many, too facile, too trivial, and too self-serving. We must insist that objectors do due diligence before we discuss a matter with them. And we need to learn to ignore them if they refuse to take centrally important and at times telling evidence in as serious a way as it deserves. Fortunately, the world contains plenty of people who will prove more willing to listen and learn.

Even strong, generally accepted theories can fail to resolve every aspect of a problem, so certain objections linger on. A perfect explanation might exist for them, but we cannot yet put our hands on it. We just have to live with imperfection and not allow ourselves to refrain from carefully considering and perhaps accepting a compelling theory just because of them. As the venture capitalists say, there's something wrong with every deal.

None of this is to say that all objections are worthless. Some prove penetrating enough to lead us to abandon a favorite hypothesis. Others help us correct mistakes. We can at times learn even from invalid ones. Still, objections are often overrated, especially by those who make them.

Insight

What role does insight play in a search for the Knowable Past? Over and over, researchers have lacked sufficient insight to spot the obvious. Velikovsky's critics did not see the perfect match between the Venus theory and the cause of the Bronze Age catastrophes. Classics scholars have not seen that Latin has a non-Indo-European grammar. Carroll Quigley's critics did not see the difference between his view of the Anglo-American Establishment and those of rightwing paranoids. Lawyer-debunkers did not see that the Kennedy assassination must have been a conspiracy. The authors of the best book on the 9/11 attacks[144] denied that there was a shred of evidence that the Bush Administration had been complicit, even though they themselves had provided various elements of the Curling Conspiracy and had perhaps encountered others. And when I first came upon the myth of Archer Yi, I immediately dismissed the notion that it might relate to the Venus theory.

Does this mean that people must have some special gift to develop insight? Generally speaking, no, though intuition certainly helps. Usually, just accumulating a store of knowledge and a set of investigative skills can give us a big advantage in regard to insight. For instance, the layout of the Karahunj stones does not necessarily instantaneously yield the outline of a raptor bird, but that doesn't mean deep insight is required to spot it. Rather, simply knowing that in China and Southeast Asia Venus was termed the Vermilion Bird makes detecting the raptor bird in Armenia a relatively easy task. In the great majority of cases, one need not be an expert or a guru to figure things out. As a psychoanalyst, Velikovsky had much experience in detecting and explaining hidden patterns in what

---

[144] Summers and Swan, 116

people were saying. That experience, rather than any deep psychic power or mastery of Freudian concepts, formed the basis of his various successes.

Thus there can be no doubt that we need sufficient insight to see the obvious or the less-than-obvious patterns in the evidence. But, given the requisite background knowledge, any intelligent college student can reasonably aspire to arrive at the kind of insights found in this book. Having a strong liberal arts background certainly helps; but even without that, a bright student could become a good detective of this sort. He or she could even construct robust, wide-ranging theories. Getting people to accept them—that's a different matter!

How We Come to Accept a Theory

Thus we need to ask, finally, what leads us to accept a theory. That has high relevance for science, history, and other fields; and it has some special twists in regard to conspiracy theories.

History has its share of conspiracies and allegations of conspiracies. In recent times the term "conspiracy theory" has become prevalent, almost invariably with a pejorative meaning as referring to something bizarre or fabricated. This fails, of course, to distinguish between a theory that accurately identifies a real conspiracy and a theory that is, unintentionally or not, wrong. So it sometimes misleads, on purpose or inadvertently. Thus it is a lamentable term. But we have to live with it. Therefore, we need to pay special attention to how we establish our own credibility, as well as to how we phrase and present our own hypotheses or theories, whether about conspiracies or not. We also need to contend with the pyrrhonists who would like us to believe that we will never know which theories are correct and which are wrong.

Various criteria exist for rating hypotheses and theories. Philosopher Peter Lipton offered a set, of which perhaps the most persuasive is *variety in the sources of supporting evidence*. Variety reduces the likelihood of idiosyncratic defects in evidence and permits us to triangulate the truth, so to speak.

A second valuable criterion, not on Lipton's list, is the *ability to resolve key anomalies*. What formed the Pacific Basin, with its Ring of Fire and seismic anomalies extending down to 2700 km below the surface? If a theory answers this in a way that closely matches the evidence, who can deny that it gains in credibility?

Many scientists are fond of a third criterion: the *ability to predict*. Velikovsky correctly predicted that Venus was hot and that Jupiter emitted radio signals, yet opponents found ways to dismiss both predictions as original contributions. Also, how does one handle a retroactive prediction, e.g., once we understand that Khrushchev's cursing referred to Mary Meyer, we could predict that the KGB would murder her. What value lies in that? Perhaps some, but how much? Besides, predictions are not always available. They refer to events that have not yet occurred. And a theory could persuade without them. Still, we can readily grasp the influence that a successful prediction has on scientists and others.

It would be good to add a fourth criterion: *expert consensus*. But so often the experts reject a breakthrough discovery—a very different kind of consensus! Yet they have skills and knowledge that could greatly aid us in advancing in the new direction. A sad paradox. Still, fairly often experts get things right, and then their agreement seems especially persuasive. Egyptologists unanimously reject the speculation that the pyramids of Giza and the Great Sphinx were built thousands of years before the third millennium BC, and we should listen carefully to their learned arguments. Ordinarily, therefore, we do well to respect experts and benefit from their knowledge. But sometimes we need to question what they say and to seek wisdom elsewhere. When to do so? The greater our knowledge, experience, and skills, the better we can discern that the experts do not have the right answer this time, let alone at all times. If all else fails, we can refrain from passing judgment.

Fifth, sometimes the best way of determining whether a theory makes sense is: *do more research*. The passage of time permits reassessment, uncovering of new evidence, application of novel research techniques, and the arrival of a new generation of researchers. Hardly surprising that over time the correct solution may emerge. It took me 22 years to work out the Trojan Origin of Roman Civilization from the moment that I perceived that Turkish bore an uncanny resemblance to Latin.

We know, at any rate, that theories tend to gain acceptance gradually as more evidence accumulates, as opponents slowly fall silent or pass away, and as a new generation with more information and more receptive minds comes to the fore. Yet this process doesn't actually guarantee that the newly accepted theory is correct. The growing acceptance of the Giant Impact hypothesis of the origin of the Earth-Moon system has now reached the point where it is fairly regularly cited in popular science literature and even in some professional journals as scientific truth. But some scientists have always held that it is wrong, and we now know *why* it is wrong!

Nor can we blithely suppose that identifying true conspiracies within the Kennedy assassination case or the 9/11 attacks will return us to a state of trust in government. Perhaps quite the contrary, many—and not just Americans—will feel confirmed in their mistrust of government!

Still, reaching a single, agreed-upon, correct (or much-more-likely-than-not) explanation of history, whether ancient or modern, can help us to achieve a more accurate, more realistic, and more complete understanding of the world around us. That is surely a sign of intellectual wellbeing, as well as a guide to dealing with the challenges we face.

Further Reading

Here are some places to start to learn more about the topics in this book.

Planetary and Earth Science

In the vast literature on planetary and Earth science, one can find pieces of evidence and snatches of theory that point in the direction of the Outer Solar System Origin of the Terrestrial Planets and the Martian Theory of Mass Extinctions. But OSSO and MTME are still new. Eventually they will attract attention and research. Meanwhile, valuable sources include articles in *Science* and *Nature* journals as well as articles and images in the NASA website: https://www.nasa.gov.

The Venus Theory

Velikovsky's *Worlds in Collision* (New York: Macmillan/Doubleday, 1950) and *Earth in Upheaval* (New York: Doubleday, 1955) remain fundamental, though they contain some errors and are out of date in various ways. Michael D. Gordin, *The Pseudoscience Wars: Immanuel Velikovsky and the Birth of the Modern Fringe* (Chicago: University of Chicago Press, 2012) provides the best treatment of the Velikovsky controversy even though it misses the great contributions of Velikovsky. Henry Bauer, *Beyond Velikovsky: The History of a Public Controversy* (Urbana IL: University of Illinois, 1984) is an earlier study, very critical of Velikovsky's science yet not completely dismissive. The leading book on the Velikovsky side is Charles Ginenthal, *Carl Sagan and Immanuel Velikovsky* (Tempe AZ: Falcon, 1995). On the Theory of the Reversing Earth, see Peter Warlow, *The Reversing Earth* (London: Dent, 1982). Of interest are articles in journals, *Pensée* and *Kronos*, published by Velikovsky's followers, and various publications of the Society for Interdisciplinary Studies.

The Trojan Origin of Roman Civilization (TORC)

Every history of Greece and Rome treats aspects of this subject. See, for example, Simon Price and Peter Thonemann, *The Birth of Classical Europe* (New York: Penguin, 2011). Alas! They and others still adhere to the continuity thesis that rejects an Etruscan invasion of Italy (p. 73).

Strategic Mistakes in the World Wars

Alexander Watson, Ring of Steel: *Germany and Austria-Hungary in World War I* (New York: Basic Books, 2014) is a thoughtful guide to World War I from a Central European perspective. Max Hastings, *Inferno: The World at War, 1939-1945* (New York: Vintage, 2012) offers an incisive, comprehensive account.

Carroll Quigley

See Quigley's *The Evolution of Civilizations* (New York: Macmillan, 1961) and *Tragedy and Hope: A History of the World in Our Time* (New York: Macmillan, 1966).

The Kennedy Assassination

The KGB theory is set forth in Ion Mihai Pacepa, *Programmed to Kill: Lee Harvey Oswald, the KGB, and the Kennedy Assassination* (Chicago: Ivan R. Dee, 2007). The best books by the debunkers are Vincent Bugliosi, *Four Days in November: The Assassination of President John F. Kennedy* (New York: W.W. Norton, 2007) and Gerald Posner, *Case*

Closed: Lee Harvey Oswald and the Assassination of JFK (New York: Anchor Books, 1993).

9/11

The most reliable general narrative is Anthony Summers and Robbyn Swan, *The Eleventh Day: The Full Story of 9/11* (New York: Ballantine Books, 2012). Of participants' accounts, the best is Richard A. Clarke, *Against All Enemies: Inside America's War on Terror* (New York: Free Press, 2004). Much useful detail can be found in The National Commission on Terrorist Attacks, *The 9/11 Commission Report* (New York: W.W. Norton, 2004). But not the real inside story….

The 2001 Anthrax Mailings Case

The printed literature falls far short or is misleading. Good sources online are https://caseclosedbylewweinstein.wordpress.com and https://vault.fbi.gov/Amerithrax.

Photo Credits

1. Unknown source
2. NASA/Johns Hopkins University Applied Physics Laboratory/Carnegie Institution of Washington
3. NASA, mosaic of images by Lunar Reconnaissance Orbiter
4. Wikimedia Commons
5. Wikimedia Commons
6. Wikimedia Commons
7. Unknown source
8. Norman Lockyer, *The Dawn of Astronomy*
9. Unknown source
10. Wikimedia Commons
11. Gérard Ducher, from the Temple at Kom Ombo, Creative Commons
12. Hedwig Storch, Wikimedia Commons. My thanks to Gary Gilligan for this.
13. Unknown source, from Susa
14. Creative Commons
15. Unknown source
16. Unknown source
17. http://www.travelarmenia.am
18. Paris M. Herouni, *Armenians and Old Armenia: Archaeoastronomy, Linguistics, Oldest History* (Yerevan: Tigran Mets, 2004)
19. J. Ollé, Wikimedia Commons
20. Unknown source
21. Kenneth J. Dillon
22. Kenneth J. Dillon
23. Kenneth J. Dillon
24. Anthony Johnson, Wikimedia Commons
25. Creative Commons
26. Unknown source
27. Unknown source
28. Wikipedia Commons
29. Unknown source
30. Domesday Book, 1969, Georgetown University
31. Dallas Police
32. Cecil Stoughton, U.S. Army
33. U.S. Department of Justice
34. The Frederick *News-Post*

Index

Able Danger 140
Abu Simbel 48, 63
Adena culture 100
Africa 26, 45
Akhenaten 58
al-Bahr mosque 67
Alibek, Ken 151-154
al Qaeda 130-132, 139, 140, 141, 142-166, 175, 177, 178
Al-Timimi, Ali 150, 154, 155
Al-'Uzza 65, 73
Amenhotep III 59
America *see* United States
American Airlines Flight #587 141, 143, 146, 147, 150, 146, 147, 157, 175
American Association for the Advancement of Science 7
AMERITHRAX *see* anthrax mailings
Amerithrax Investigative Summary 158-162
Amun 46, 59, 60
Ancient Near East 64-71
Angleton, James 131
Anglo-American Establishment 119, 122-123, 173, 179
anthrax mailings 130, 138, 141, 142-166, 175, 176-177, 178
antipodal disruption 20, 24, 26, 38, 45
Anuket 59
Anyang 42
Aphrodite 12, 75
Apophis 60
Arab 42, 67-68
archaeoastronomy 14, 68, 94, 98, 170
archaeology 9, 46, 99
Archer Yi *see* Yi, Archer
Ares 83
Argentina 37
Armenia 68-71
Asherah 64-65
Ashur 64, 65, 68
Assyria 65
Astarte 64, 72-74, 75

asteroid 16, 19, 30
Aswan 59
Athena 12, 73, 74, 75, 83, 168
Atlantis 50
Atta, Mohamed 140, 143, 144, 145, 146, 147, 150, 153, 154, 155, 164
'Attar/'Astar 64
Ayet 59
axial tilt 28
Aztecs 47, 61, 95, 97

Babylonians 46, 66-67, 73
Bailey, Charles 151-156
ballgame, Mesoamerican 98
Bamboo Annals 82, 85
Barrancas del Cobre 33
Bastet 59
Battle of Britain 115
Beaker Ware people 92-93
Bible 170
Black Drop 17
Borealis Planitia 25
Bronze Age 14, 31, 37, 39, 42, 45, 46, 69, 103
Bronze Age catastrophes 4, 5, 14, 15, 37, 43, 44, 62, 65, 92, 170, 179
Buckyballs 39
Bugliosi, Vincent 174, 179
bull of heaven 46, 51, 65, 67, 69, 73, 76, 77, 100
Bush, George W. 138-139, 157, 175, 176

calendrics 9
celestial mechanics 39
center of mass 28-29
Cheney, Dick 139, 157, 175, 176
Chicxulub 32, 37
China 37, 46, 70, 78-87, 116, 179
   ten-sun episode 47
Chi You 83
chronology, revised 6, 10-11, 58

CIA (Central Intelligence Agency) 126-127, 131-132, 134, 135
circularization of orbits 7, 9, 18, 19, 21, 67
civilization 120-121, 123
Clarke, Richard 140
climate change 41, 78-87, 170
Clinton, Bill 118-120, 123, 139
comet 12, 16, 20, 22
   Earth 24
   Mars 24, 86
   short-term 19
   tail 12, 16, 17, 18, 20, 21, 23, 24, 46, 59, 61, 75, 77, 84, 86, 90, 97, 100, 101, 167
   Venus 12, 13, 19, 29, 46, 51, 52, 58, 60, 61, 62, 64, 66, 67, 69, 70, 71, 74, 75, 76, 77, 84, 89, 90, 94, 96, 97, 99, 100, 167, 168
Conan Doyle, Arthur 10
conspiracy theory 122, 138, 171-175, 179, 180, 182
Copernicus 5
Cretaceous-Tertiary (KT) extinction 32
Crete 70, 72-76
Crump, Raymond, Jr. 130-132
Cuban Missile Crisis 124-126, 132-137, 174
cultural amnesia 52, 86-87, 96, 170
Curling Conspiracy 140, 175, 179
Cyprus 75

Dawn of Astronomy, The 55
Daoism 86
DARPA (Defense Advanced Research Projects Agency) 141, 150, 154
Daschle, Tom 145, 151, 152, 164
Deccan Traps 32
Defense Department, U.S. 120, 139-140, 151, 153, 156, 159, 162
Dej, Gheorghe *see* Gheorghiu-Dej, Gheorghe
dendrochronology 47
density, uncompressed 29
Destruction of Men, The 61
deuterium:hydrogen ratio 16, 17
Devonian, Late extinction 38
Distant Goddess, The 60
Dorian 105, 106, 172
Doubleday 5, 6

dragon 85, 86, 100
Duley, Jean 159-160
Durrington Walls 91
Dushara 64

Earth 5, 7, 15-18, 21, 23-30, 33-40, 41-47, 50, 62, 65-66, 84-86, 91, 93, 95, 97-98, 167-170, 178
   Earth-Moon system 19
   as comet 24
Earth in Upheaval 6
earthquakes 5, 33, 77, 80, 89, 90, 92
Earth science 3, 4, 6, 13
eclipse 66-67
Edfu 59
Egypt 48-62, 66, 168
Egyptian priests 8, 41, 47
Egyptologists 49-50, 62, 181
Einstein, Albert 6
electromagnetic forces 6, 8, 10, 12, 18, 42
Elysium Mons 34
epagomenal days 60
Erechthion 77
Erlitou, 79, 85
Etruscans 44, 102-110, 171
Evening Star 53, 59, 61, 70-71, 84, 91-92, 96-98
extinctions *see* mass extinctions
Eye of Ra 58-61

Faint Young Sun Paradox 27
fast precession 43-45
Fellows, Patricia F. 152-153, 155, 156
Fenus 75
Fira 75
Flame Emperor (*Yandi*) 85
flood 5, 9, 37, 42, 66, 79, 80, 85, 87, 89, 92
flood basalt 24, 35, 36
4.2 ka event 81, 92
Franz, David 153-156

Galileo 5
geology 9
geomagnetic field *see* magnetic field
geomagnetic reversal 43
George Mason University 141, 150, 153-154, 156

Getman, Ross 150, 163
Gheorghiu-Dej, Gheorghe 125-126, 135-136
giant impact *see* Mars, Mercury, Moon
Gilgamesh 73, 77
Ginsberg, Allen 134-136
Gong Gong 85
Grand Canyon 33
gravity 8, 10, 12, 15, 19, 20, 36, 42
Great Britain 111-117
Great Pyramid *see* Pyramid, Great
Great Sphinx *see* Sphinx, Great
Greeks 12, 29, 42, 44, 72-77, 102-105
Greenland *see* ice cores
Guru (Jupiter) 12

Hadley, Stephen 140
Hadron 153, 156
Haj 67
Hammurabi, stele of 66
Hatfill, Steven 148, 165
Hathor 51, 57, 58, 59, 61, 64, 168
Hatshepsut 55
Hawkins, Gerald 55
Hellas Basin 25, 38
Herakleopolis 59
Herodotus 9, 41, 47
Hindenburg, Paul von 172
Hindus 12
Hitler, Adolf 114, 122, 172
Homer 73, 103
Horus 42, 49, 54, 57, 60
hotspots, Hawaiian and South Pacific 26, 27, 45
Huainanzi 84, 85
Huangdi see Yellow Emperor
human sacrifice 83, 84, 97, 170
Hungarian 102, 107

ice cores, Greenland 9-10
iconography 9, 17, 27, 51, 52, 170
Iliad 83, 97, 103
impact, bolide 37, 45
impact, giant *see* Mars, Mercury, Moon
Inanna 64
Indian Ocean 116
Inferior Conjunction 61, 91, 98
insight 179-180

in situ formation 28, 170
Internet 7
inversion 8-9, 11, 27, 37, 39, 40-47, 53-58, 66, 68, 70, 78, 82, 92, 93, 95, 97, 168, 178
Iraq War 139-140
Iron Age 39, 103
Ishtar 64, 65, 66, 73, 75
Isis 51, 52, 59, 60, 73, 74
Islam 67-68
Israel 139-140
Ivins, Bruce 141, 149, 150-166, 177

Jabarah, Mohammed Mansour 142, 146, 150
Japan 115-117, 172
Jason 26
Jdey, Abderraouf 141-157, 177
Jingwei Bird 85
Jupiter 5, 7, 12, 13, 15, 16, 17, 19, 22, 24, 27, 28, 29, 30, 31, 44, 64, 68, 167-169, 181

Kaaba 67
Karahunj 68-71, 179
Karnak, Temple of Amun-Re at 46, 54-58
Kennedy, John F. 3, 124-136, 167, 171, 173-174, 175, 178, 179, 182
KGB 124-137
Khafre (Cephren) 49-53
Khrushchev, Nikita 125-126, 129, 132-136, 181
Khufu (Cheops) 49, 50, 51, 53
Kilgallen, Dorothy 129
Knossos 70
Knowable Past 3
Koran 68

Lambert, Richard 149
Late Heavy Bombardment 23, 25, 30
Latin 102-108, 179, 182
Latinii 106-110
lava *see* flood basalts
Leahy, Patrick 145, 146, 151, 164
Leary, Timothy 134
Lemnos 103, 104, 105
Liangzhu Culture 79, 81
linguistics, 9

Lipton, Peter 180-181
Lockyer, Norman 55-56
Longshan Culture 46, 79-80, 81, 83
Ludendorff, Erich 172
Luwian, 110

Macmillan 5, 6
Magliano disk 109
magnetic field
  Earth 25-26, 44
  Mars 25
  Mercury 20, 22
  Moon 25
Mars 8, 18, 24, 25, 26, 27, 28, 30, 31, 32-40, 44, 62, 63, 83, 86, 93, 97, 98, 169, 178
Martian Theory of Mass Extinctions (MTME) 32-40, 45, 169, 178
mass extinctions 32-40, 45, 167
Master Impression of Chania (Kydonia) 77
Mayan 95, 97
Mayan calendar 65
McLean, Judith 159-160
Mecca 67
Menhaure 50, 51, 168
Merculuna 19, 22, 23, 27
Mercury 16, 18-25, 28, 29, 51
Mesoamerica 95-99
Mesopotamia 66, 96
Metis 12, 168
Meyer, Cord 126-127, 131, 134
Meyer, Mary 125-136, 174, 187
Minoan 70, 72-74
Minotaur 76
Mirovia Ocean 26
Mohamed, Prophet 67, 164
Mohammed, Khalid Sheikh 142-143
Moon 17, 18, 20, 21, 24, 28, 335, 46, 66-67, 90, 92, 93
  as comet 29, 20, 21, 23
  capture of 20-22, 23, 24
  Giant Impact hypothesis 22, 23, 24, 27, 31, 170, 182
  Mars approach 38
Morning Star 53, 59, 61, 70, 91, 96, 97
Moundbuilders 101
Moussaoui, Zacarias 143, 147, 150
Mushtaree 64, 68

Mut 59
Mycenaeans 76, 103
myth 8, 9, 11, 12, 13, 29, 31, 41, 42, 66, 79, 84, 86, 97, 170, 173

Nabataeans 64
National Academy of Sciences (NAS) 151-152, 162
NASA (National Aeronautics and Space Agency) 20
Nefertari 48, 52, 63, 74
Nehemtawy 59
Neptune, 17
Nibiru 65
Nilsson, Martin 75
9/11 2001 attacks 138-141, 143, 144, 145, 149, 153, 155, 157, 163, 167, 175, 179, 182
Nosenko, Yurii 128, 174

Objection 8, 9, 35-36, 42, 177-179
Objection Game 9, 13, 178
Oceanus Procellarum 20, 21, 31
Olmec 95, 96
opportunistic facilitation 140, 176
orbit
  eccentricity 18, 21, 23, 25
  inclination 28
Orion 50
Osiris 62
Oswald, Lee Harvey 124, 126, 127, 128, 174, 175
outer solar system 15, 16, 22
Outer Solar System Origin of the Terrestrial Planets (OSSO) 15-31, 45, 169
oxygen ratios of Earth and Moon 19

Pacepa, Ion Mihai 125, 128, 129, 135-136, 174
Pacific Basin 24, 25, 26, 31, 44-45, 169, 181
Pacific Ocean 22, 26, 27, 43, 44, 45, 79, 115, 116
Parameter Game 9, 178
Pearl Harbor 116, 175
pecked-cross circles 96
Peripheral Passage of Jupiter 12-13, 22, 23, 27, 28, 29

Permian extinction 38
Phaistos disk 108-110
Phoenicia 75
planetary science 3, 4, 6, 9, 13
Plato 42, 44, 119
Popov, Sergei 154
Portland, Maine 144, 145, 147, 148
Poseidon 76-77, 168
Posner, Gerald 174, 179
pseudoscience 5, 11
Ptah 59
Pyramid, Great 49, 53
Pyramid of the Moon 97
Pyramid of the Sun 97

Quetzalcoatl 97, 98
Quigley, Carroll 118-123, 173, 179
Qing dynasty 86

Ra (Re) 60, 61
radiation pressure 15
Ramses II 48, 56, 63, 74
Red Pearl 85
Red Star 97
Re-Horakhty 41, 49, 53-54, 56
Reid, Richard 148
Reimer Gamma Formation 21
Reversing Earth, The 43
Reversing Earth, Theory of the 11, 14, 15, 41-47, 167-170
Ring of Fire 26, 31, 181
RMR-1029 153, 154, 155, 158-159, 163
Roche limit 40
Romans 75, 102, 106-110, 171
Rosicrucians 65
Royal Navy 111
Round Table *see* Angle-American Establishment
Ruby, Jack 129, 174
Russia 111-113

Saathof, Gregory 160
Sabbath Queen 68
Sagan, Carl 13
Salkeld, David 43
San Lorenzo 96-97
Santorini (Thera) 75, 77

Satet 59
Saturn 7, 17, 30
Scarlet Lady 61
Schlieffen Plan 112
Schoch, Robert 50, 53
scientific rejectionism 4, 6, 7, 8, 14, 87, 167
secondary equator 43
See, Thomas Jackson Jefferson 17
Sekhmet 58-62
Senenmut (Senmut) 42
Serabit el Khadim 57
Serpent Mound, Great 98-101
Seth 62
Shamash 66
Shang dynasty 46, 47, 79-80, 81, 82, 83, 85, 86
Shiva 12
Shoemaker-Levy-9 comet 12
Shukra 12
Silbury Hill 89
silicon 151-152, 154, 156
Sitchin, Zecharia 8
Slabinski, Victor 43
Slushball Earth 34
snake goddess 72-74, 75
snow line 15, 30
solar wind 15, 30, 70, 85, 90
South Atlantic Magnetic Anomaly 26
South Pole-Aitken Basin 28
Southern Research Institute (SRI) 152, 153, 154, 156
Soviet Union 114-116, 124-136, 151, 154, 164
Sphinx, Great 48-54, 61, 168, 181
Sphinx Temple 53
SRI *see* Southern Research Institute
Stecchini, Livio 7
Stonehenge 10, 46, 52, 70, 88-94, 168
stratigraphic record, gaps in 34
Study in Scarlet, A 10
submarine warfare, unrestricted 113
Sun 15, 18, 19, 27, 28, 30, 41, 42, 46, 47, 49, 52-60, 61, 66, 69-71, 85, 90, 93, 97, 98, 168
  western-rising 41-47, 53-58, 66, 67, 71, 80, 82, 83-84, 85, 86, 92, 93, 95, 96, 98
Superior Conjunction 61

Syria 65

Tanis 57
Taosi 70-71, 83, 84
Tefnut 59
Teotihuacan 95, 98
Terramars 24, 25, 26, 27, 44, 169
terrestrial planets 13, 15-30
terrorism 138-141, 142-166, 167, 174-176
Tezcatlipoca 97
Tharsis region 33, 36, 39
Thebes, Egypt 55
Thira (Thera) see Santorini
tidal forces 8, 12, 16, 19, 21, 22, 34, 35, 36, 69
tidal locking 17, 29, 36
tin 151-156
tippe top 43
Tlaloc/Chac 97
Toltec 95
torture policy, U.S. 139
Tragedy and Hope 120-122
Trojan 4, 83, 102-110, 170-172
Trojan Origin of Roman Civilization (TORC) 4, 102-110, 170-172, 182
True Polar Wander 26, 27
tsunami 9, 32, 34, 37, 42, 45, 78, 79, 81, 82, 86, 87, 89
Tuthmosis III 56
Tuzo 26

Uffington, White Horse of 100
Ugric 102, 103, 107, 108, 110
United States 4, 121, 124-137, 138-141
uraeus 60
Uranus 17
USAMRIID (United States Army Research Institute of Infectious Diseases) 151, 152, 153, 154, 159
U-2 flights 127

Valles Marineris 33
Van Allen radiation belt 26
varves 46
Velikovsky, Immanuel 4, 5-14, 15, 29, 31, 42, 50, 58, 74, 78, 86, 97, 98, 99, 167-170, 177, 178, 179, 180, 181

biography 6
Freudian psychoanalyst 6
scholarly malpractice 10
Venus
 approaches 9, 10, 11, 14, 37, 39, 42, 46, 50-51, 69-71, 88-94, 95-101
 characteristics 17, 29, 30, 31, 58-62, 181
 orbit 9, 18
 ovoid 11, 17, 18, 27-28, 52, 58, 60, 65, 69, 89 93, 95, 100, 168
 proto-Venus 12, 13
 retrograde rotation 17, 29, 168
 Theory 4, 5-14, 42, 65, 78, 87, 88, 97, 98, 99, 101, 167-170, 178, 179
Vermilion Bird 69, 85, 179-180
volcano 33, 34, 36, 37, 38, 39, 53, 80, 89
Von Däniken, Erich 8
vowel harmony 108

Warlow, Peter 27, 42
water
 Mars 24
 Moon 22
 origin and distribution 15, 16, 30
 water ice of Mercury 20
Western Civilization 108, 119-123
western-rising Sun see Sun
Wilhelm II, Kaiser 113, 172
winged disk 65
Wolfowitz, Paul 139, 175
Woodhenge 92
Worlds in Collision 5, 6, 43-44, 78, 98, 177
World War I 4, 111-113, 172
World War II 4, 114-117, 172
www.scientiapress.com 4

Xia dynasty 46, 79-80, 81, 82, 83, 85, 86, 87

Yao, Emperor 83
Yellow Emperor 83, 85
Yi, Archer 46, 84, 85, 86, 90, 168, 179
Yü dynasty 80
Yueshi 79

Zeus see Jupiter
Zhou dynasty 47, 80, 81, 82, 83
Zimmermann telegram 113

About the Author

Kenneth J. Dillon earned a Ph.D in history from Cornell University in 1973, has taught European history at several universities, and has served as a foreign service officer and intelligence analyst (two prizes for analysis). Since leaving the State Department, Dillon has worked as a theoretical scientist, medical writer, entrepreneur, and historian.

Among Dillon's life science contributions are theories of the red blood cells' role in consciousness, of shared mechanisms of various natural remedies, and of transdermal micronutrition. He has also formulated an 18-point proof that the red blood cells constitute the animal magnetoreceptor.

In planetary science, Dillon has interpreted myths and scientific data to explain why Venus seemed to emerge from Jupiter. He has also devised a theory of the origins of Mercury, Venus, Mars, the Moon, and Earth, including the Pacific Basin. Another theory argues that approaches of Mars led to the great mass extinctions.

In ancient history, Dillon has formulated a theory of the relationships among Trojans, Etruscans, and Romans that explains how the Greeks won the Trojan War and why Latin has an Ugric grammar. He has also provided apposite explanations of Stonehenge, the Great Serpent Mound, the stele of Hammurabi, the Minoan Snake Goddess, the Phaistos disk, the Master Impression of Kydonia, the lioness goddess Sekhmet, the Great Sphinx, and the temple at Karnak. He has found the origins of the names Ishtar/Astarte, Dorian, Athena, Poseidon, and Venus. And he has identified China's original Yellow Emperor and the *modus operandi* of Archer Yi in shooting down nine of ten suns.

In modern history, Dillon has identified how Nikita Khrushchev was misled into undertaking his reckless Cuban missile adventure, and he has contributed a new angle that supports a nuanced KGB theory of the assassination of John F. Kennedy. He has also shown that al Qaeda operative Abderraouf Jdey was the likely mailer of the 2001 anthrax letters.

According to the Minnesota Multiphasic Personality Inventory, Dillon is normal but with a tendency to be naively trusting (!). One interpretation would be that, when one theorizes, such a psychological profile conduces to balance (normal) even as one pays attention (trusting) to information that could otherwise be prematurely ruled out. As his efforts to master technical detail invariably fall short, Dillon focuses on detecting underlying patterns and devising explanations for them. He is a special projects guy, a historical and scientific detective.

Dillon is a student of international affairs and psychology, an amateur linguist and musician, and a member of the American Association for the Advancement of Science.